I Am JOY

Joy M. England

I Am Joy

13th & Joan Publishing

I Am Joy. Copyright 2019 by Joy M. England. All rights reserved. No part of this publication may be reproduced, distributed, or transmitted in any form or by any means, including photocopying, recording, or other electronic or mechanical methods, without the prior written permission of the publisher, except in the case of brief quotations embodied in critical reviews and certain other noncommercial uses permitted by copyright law. For permission requests, write to the publisher, addressed "Attention: Permissions Coordinator," 500 N. Michigan Avenue, Suite #600, Chicago, IL 60611.

13th & Joan books may be purchased for educational, business or sales promotional use. For information, please email the Sales Department at sales@13thandjoan.com.

First Edition Printed, July 2019

Library of Congress Cataloging-in-Publication Data has been applied for.

ISBN: 978-1-7331313-1-5

I Am Joy

TO MY BOYS:

You have no idea the light and love you shown into a very sad and darkened heart. I thank you for your love, your laughs, and your hugs over the years. Owen, your bravery and strength is truly a gift from God and just a few of the reasons why I am in awe of you daily. Nate, my partner in crime, you are nothing short of amazing; thank you for being the toughest, wisest young man I have known. Chase your dreams boys, even when it's the scariest thing to do— that's when it matters most. It's been a tough road at times; I hope that you have always felt safe in this little family of ours. I pray you go on to honor your stories as the best thing you can bring to this world is you.

TO SAMANTHA:

What can I say to the little girl who brightened all of our lives that fall day in 1995. You were the first person to ever show me what love feels like. I grew to love you like a daughter; even though in many ways you became the sister that I always longed for. I admire you more than you will ever know. Keep believing in you no matter what; you are the definition of a conqueror.

Contents

I Am Joy 5

INTRO By Joy M. England 7

1 My very first I Am's 9

2 I Am An Adult 23

3 What If 47

4 I Am Saved 77

INTRO

By Joy M. England

We have all asked ourselves the infamous question of "who am I, why am I here, what does it all mean? Well as we hurl ourselves down this journey of life—it feels more like a free fall off of a cliff at times—we will come to answer our ever-looming question of just who we are over and over.

In that current moment, the answer to who we are is profoundly important. It is all those who am I's that becomes the person, woman, mother, friend, wife, and career woman that stands before you in the mirror today.

So many times, the answer of who am I made me shudder; it brought deep shame and opened the floodgates for self-loathing talk that could marvel even the darkest minds. (I have mastered the art of here is how you suck, let's count the ways" thinking). I carried these answers as scars—proof if you will—that I was a lost cause. No matter how much I would accomplish, nothing washed away all the many reasons I firmly believed made me inherently flawed; it was this think-

- I Am Joy -

ing that, sadly for decades of my life, forced me to answer the question of "Who I am" with this answer: shattered.

    I have come to love my I AM's; they are my stripes, my badges, my reminders that I never stop fighting, I never stop working, even when I believed I would never be worthy of anything. There was a dim, almost extinguished, light that burned deep in the essence of who I was created to be; that ever-so-quiet-but-steady light kept me pushing forward. Boy am I thankful for that light, I can say now, as I type these pages to an audience that I am amazed will exist one day. That my little light is now a beacon, guiding not only me, but all who I encounter in this amazing, sometimes gnarly, journey of life.

1

My very first I Am's

Growing up Joy. What a weird, Lifetime Movie chronicle my life has been. To say that I grew up confused, a bit lost, and a lot terrified would be an understatement of epic proportions. I have two awesome parents. Parents that did all they knew to do with a lot in the parenthood life that parallels some of the best Hollywood dramas. It is hard enough being parents, let alone parents who were chartering territory that was littered with landmines.

Dramatic, you say? If only I was being overdramatic. We all have our tales of wo. For me, I seemed to be born into mine, and spent the majority of my life trying to figure out what I had done in another life to deserve what seemed to be perpetual torture and tragedy. It wouldn't be until I came to know and accept Christ into my heart, that I could realize the majesty that was this story. That, like any fairytale, there must tears in order to have triumph. My triumphs would be many, albeit I wouldn't be able to acknowledge them as such until many decades later. So let's take a peek in to the beginnings that

- *I Am Joy* -

shaped the woman who ended up being braver than any woman she had ever dreamed she could be.

    I am the youngest of two children, born to parents who fought to make a life and name for themselves, separate of what their individual family trees would say they could be. My sister is six years my senior, and from what I can imagine(being a mother myself now) she was likely none too thrilled to be welcoming a crying baby into her world. But! As we all know, sometimes life doesn't go how we think it should. Here is what I will say about my sister: I love her. She is my big sister, the person I wanted desperately to be liked and loved by, for the majority of my life. She is smart and funny and caring, when she feels compelled to be. She is the mother of my nieces, and for that I am ever grateful to her. She taught me a lot about life. She showed me, as big sisters do, what is good and what is bad, how to act and treat people, and how not to act and treat people. My sister was never my friend, but she was my teacher, and I think in many ways I was hers. As a Christian, I know without a shadow of uncertainty: we are all destined, we all have a purpose, we all have a reason for being in this world. I believe this to be true of every last one of us. I also know that it is not up to me to judge what is right and wrong in the actions of another. If I had penned these pages just a few years ago, this storyline narrative would be very different. As we all must in life, we have to forgive, we have to take our lives and know that we were given this life because we were the ones chosen for the job. So, to my sister who is forging her own path in this world, I pray she has found her meaning in the crazy life she was destined, and I will forever be grateful for your teachings. Her role in my life had intense impact; it shaped me and changed me. You will see her presence in much of my story as I described Who I AM, and how I began to define my very first I Am's.

- Joy M. England -

As we travel down these winding and treacherous roads in our destined journey, we are always looking for definitions of who we are, especially to my friends out there who have had a particularly treacherous road in this journey. I have come to see that these definitions become labels we cover ourselves with. If we aren't careful, we will cover ourselves with so many labels that are expired, out of date, and no longer valid that there is no room for the current labels—the labels with absolute truth in their meaning. My story is not much different from anyone else's. We all struggle, we all fail, we are all hurt, we are all broken. BUT the good news is that we are also saved, called, marked, forgiven, and redeemed. My prayer is that my story of how I was able to let go of those expired I AM labels and picked up my current, powerful I AM labels will help to set you free from your expired labels.

I often wonder at what point do we decide that we suck? Is there a precise moment where our world, path, family, choices, perceptions tell us, "Yep, sorry kid, but you suck"? I think for me, this was a cumulative event; because I didn't feel I had a voice that was audible to anyone. As a child, I internalized my world as, "You are too insignificant to be noticed. You are so unimportant that even your cries can't be heard." Feeling unchosen was the theme to my entire life. I accepted that as my fate as a small child, and I carried that as armor through most of my life. It manifested in different ways throughout my life, but the underlying belief was always, "Try as you might but no one will choose you." Sadly, the person who I desperately needed to choose me...was me.

I have two main ways I remember myself as a child. The first is me at age—geez—probably 8, in my First Communion dress; as I type this I am just now realizing the significance of that. Anyway, picture a brown-haired child with bangs that would make Shannen Doherty, in the early Brenda Walsh years, envious. With an innocent (albeit tremendously sad) smile. It is this Joy that my psyche holds onto. She was and is significant. She's a survivor. She's a warrior who had no idea the battles before her, and certainly had no idea of the strength buried inside her. The other version of myself that is associated with my formative years would be my early teens: big hair, , a New Kids on the Block sweatshirt with matching...well, everything. I was a 90's teen. Awkward phases: we all have them. Mine seemed to be the world's worst but looking back, it was just your average awkward teenage phase. As I became an adult, there were several other versions of myself that I would come to immortalize in my mind.

Communion dress Joy. Who was she and why was she important? She was the embodiment of the confusion that I felt. I was in this environment that I couldn't understand, that I couldn't predict. I had no refuge from the pain and sorrow that surrounded me. But still, I got up, put on the dress, and smiled. Those skills of hiding and lying to myself would come to be the fortress that I remained behind until my late 30s. I am sure at this point you are asking yourselves, "Why was she so sad and tortured?" Well the long and short answer to that is mental health issues and struggles suck.

My childhood home was beautiful, immaculate, and always supplied the needs a house should: shelter and sustenance. I never had material lack as a child; my parents worked hard to provide my sister and I with a life that would be the envy of many. It was wonderful. I was blessed, and I learned many many things about work ethic, persistence, and making your own way from watching my parents. That same house was also a prison for all of us: we lived behind lock and key, trauma and chaos at every turn. I learned that unrest and fear were the norm. My sister struggles with significant mental health issues. I am no psychiatrist, so I will not proclaim a diagnosis. I will, however, tell my story from my perspective. The derivative of my sister's issues is not a factor in telling my story; the importance of her life struggles is. The power her issues had over my destiny and story are paramount in understanding who I am. My sister made life hard—unbearable at times. There was always unrest. There was always fear. There was always torment. My sister stole, it's what she did. So, we lived behind locked doors inside our home to protect us, feebly. As an adult I realized that since I grew up always being robbed, I became an adult that would hold onto things so strongly, for fear that one day I would wake up and they would have disappeared. That became a coping skill that was detrimental to me in so many ways for many years. I developed a hatred for my sister, my life, my upbringing, and sadly at times, for my parents. This hatred for my sister sat juxtaposed to my desire to be loved by her. I just wanted her to love me as much as I wanted her to leave and never come back. The purpose of me sharing my life isn't to throw shade on my sister; judgement is not mine to give, but forgiveness is. I forgive her. I accept her. She is and will always be an important part of my story, because in large part, it was her teachings that shaped the woman of Christ I am today. July 2006 was the last time I spoke to my sister, as my youngest son turned 3. I captioned what, at the time I didn't realize was, an immensely brave move for a very broken me. I sent an email that said, "I love you because you are my sister, but I choose not to have a relationship with you because you are too toxic to me." This declaration came not because I was overtly protecting myself; I was overtly protecting the people that taught me that you protect the ones you love: my boys, Owen and Nate. I hit send on that email and never looked back. It would be years of therapy, growth, healing, and deliverance that would allow me to get to a point where I could say I forgive her; and I accept my childhood as the necessary foundation for the brave, faith warrior woman I am before you now. How could I not be grateful to my sister and honor a childhood that did exactly what it was supposed to—birth a voice that would go onto to impact the lives of women.

The other version of me as a child that often runs through my mind is my pre-teen years. My sadness and tortured existence would be the theme of most of my life; the pre-teen and teen years are not fabulous for most. Mine was probably a bit stormier than the average. I grew to believe the following lies: you are unworthy, you are untalented, you are unwanted, you are unloved, you are a failure, you are ugly, you are fat, and you are weak—just to name a few. These messages would become my self talk that would take most of my first three decades of life to undo. We all survive trauma of some kind as kids, and the messages we get from those traumas can encourage or discourage. Unfortunately for me, the discouragement would become like quicksand surrounding me for years. Looking back, the hardest part for me—the part that made it so hard to emotionally recover from—was the way in which the trauma and abuse would happen at the happy times. Let me explain. I have an extremely vivid memory of my childhood home: my sister and I playing school in the unfinished basement. I could not have been more than six-years-old, which would have made her twelve. I was loving life in this moment; I was getting the attention of my sister, I was playing in a world that made sense, and I was able to shut out the hurt that was my reality. All in all, for a six-year-old, life was great in this moment. Then it changed, in an instant—my excitement and happiness was eclipsed by the evil that I had come to know all too well. I saw a look come over my sister's face, a look that I immediately recognized, and I knew it didn't mean good things. She stared into my eyes as I sat in an old high chair, pretending to be her student. Staring at me, she smirked and knocked the entire high chair to the ground, causing me to slam face first into the cement floor. As the screams and blood filled the basement, I remember distinctly thinking, "Well you must have deserved this." When my parents rushed into the basement, all I could do was agree with the story my sister had concocted, now crying for the pretend concern she had for her injured sister. "Joy did it. She knocked over the high chair. I told her not to." For years after this incident, I would have not only an emotional reminder, but a physical one: a black front tooth. I didn't know it then, but I know now, these traumas were all a necessary part of my path in this life. You see, I would need to learn as an adult that sometimes the best thing we can do is wear our scars outwardly, let the world see that we have endured, and conquered. It would be many decades later before I could learn to accept this life lesson as a blessing. Your battles and your hurts will either make you or break you—that's life. We all have to make that decision with the tools we have at the time. I most certainly had no good tools at age six, so I chose what vulnerable little girls chose: I chose to blame me because I was too scared to not be loved by my family. I wish that my childhood trauma began and ended there, but it didn't. My childhood and adolescence were peppered with events like this one. They would rob me of my voice and ability to live a fulfilling life for years. It's these moments that shape how we learn to cope, how we learn to love, how we learn to decide what we deserve, and what we are worth.

Don't get me wrong, I was not always so enlightened and forgiving. I spent many years with buried and obvious hatred and anger. It was this battle of love and hate that tore me apart from the inside out. I felt such anger towards not just my sister and my parents, but towards the extended family that ,in my mind, abandoned me. My family consisted of a good number of aunts and uncles deriving from both sides of my family. Some who lived far and some who lived a few towns away. My one aunt in particular, we will call her Jane, she was my favorite. Oh, I just loved her; I loved watching how she moved and dressed. She had such style and glamor, at least to me, as a little girl she seemed so put together. She was my cool aunt. She would do what cool aunts did: they come get you from school when your mom can't, they show you the magic that is makeup, they laugh at your jokes, and love you in a way that makes your heart leap. I remember as a little girl wanting desperately to tell Jane what life was like at home, the torture we were all enduring at the hands of my sister—I never did tell. I didn't have the skills to find that voice, and I never wanted to hurt my parents by telling the truth. Just as many things do, this relationship with my favorite aunt and uncle and their kids ended. Just ended, one day they were there and the next day they were gone. That was so sad and scary for me. I remember asking why, where they went, why couldn't we go see them, and I was never given an answer. I was the kid, and this was just how it was. In my child mind and heart, this loss came to serve as confirmation for my negative self-talk: you really are not important, everyone will leave you, you don't matter. This was my first real experience with loss and abandonment. Years later, when I was about seventeen, I wrote my aunt a letter. I told her how I loved and missed her. I will be honest, I don't really remember the entire contents of the letter. The emotion it conjures up is deep sadness. I hoped that she would respond. These were the days before email and cell phones; I wrote a letter and mailed it. It was never acknowledged. Rejected again by the family who is supposed to love you no matter what. It's amazing how the foundational experiences of life can truly set your internal beliefs. My life became about trying to figure out who would ever pick me; and life showed me that family doesn't always pick you.

As my sister grew in age, her treachery grew in magnitude. It became so far spread that that my parents struggled to hide it. We couldn't contain the wreckage anymore, the devastation poured out

— Joy M. England —

through the doors of that immaculate home and was visible for the world to see. I thought, "Yes! Finally, someone can see and help." Surely someone one would see that I was dying here and would show me the acceptance and love that I was starving for. Unfortunately for me, that is not how the story would be written. Things happen in life and sides are chosen; I was always on the unchosen side (which would come to be one of the best gifts God has ever given me). I was a teen now, so I was capable of anger and storming out, which I did regularly. I longed for my remaining extended family to see me, to hear me, to choose me; I was unsuccessful. Just more confirmation that I was never the one who someone would pick. I have since come to see that my father's siblings were trying to do what they thought was best. They were trying to help my sister (fix her, if you will) thinking that would stop the storm we all lived in, thereby helping me. Their intentions were well placed. The problem was, when you put all of your energy and resources towards extinguishing the fire, you often forget to sweep the blaze for victims. I can proclaim that I was a victim of my sister's mental health issues and my family's inability to cope with said mental health issues. What I don't accept anymore is the scarlet V on my chest. I was a victim and now I am not, and that's as simple as it needs to be. All these years later, we are still a family divided. I have not spoken to or heard one word from my favorite aunt, and with the remaining aunts and uncles, it's a social media relationship of likes and thumbs ups. By the grace of God and my therapist I have been able to heal past this. I know that they did the best they could as I did the best I could. I forgive them and most importantly I forgive myself. The stories of our lives are the bricks we build ourselves out of, and I have built myself with bricks that no weapon formed against me could break down. I thank my family. I thank them for loving me in the ways they knew how. I thank them for doing what they thought was best for themselves and their children. I thank them for being part of my story in whatever way they could. I thank them for the lessons they taught me. Most importantly, I thank them for choosing my sister, because she needs them more than I did. I will always love them; they are my blood. I will always wonder how my favorite aunt is, and I pray that they have lived beautiful lives. When my twinges of rejection and abandonment rear their ugly heads, I remind myself of this: when it mattered most, the most important person to choose me was me. I thank God I made that choice every day.

THE PARENTS

I WAS A disappointment to my parents. They deny that, but it's just the facts. Since my sister was riddled with issues, I think my parents thought that I would just do better and be better by osmosis. Life doesn't happen that way. It was unfair for them to expect a whole and functional person when my life as a child and young adult had not provided a strong foundation to sustain a full adult. Don't get me wrong here, my life was not all torture and dark nights. I love my parents; my mom and I shared many laughs and shopping days. I always wanted to be with my mom, and as she blossomed into a woman of her own; I admired her ambition. My parents had it tough. Life was tough in a lot of ways; I don't really think their marriage ever had a chance. My parents divorced when I was sixteen, and it was hard. I had the dream every kid has of their parents together and everyone and everything to be okay. I never really knew what everything being okay felt like, so I probably had a more romanticized version of that in my head than most kids. I believe in my heart that my parents did the best they could in a situation they had absolutely no knowledge base in. As a parent, I know that sometimes you are just trying to survive, and you can't always see the collateral damage. I learned a lot from my parents. My father is one of the hardest working men I have ever known. I learned what it means to work hard, provide for your family, and try to be the person everyone needs you to be. My dad tried to protect me, he tried to be the dad I needed. Sometimes as parents we just don't know what that is, and maybe we can't figure it out. What I know now is my dad tried; he did the best he could by me, and I am thankful that he taught me the things he did because they served me well in life. My mom and I were so close for so long. Things change, people grow, and life moves on. My mom and I eventually grew apart, and as an adult I had to find my way back to relationship with my parents. My relationship as an adult with parents is difficult, for a lot of reasons. Some of those reasons were valid and some are not. Unbeknownst to me, I carried a lot of hurt and pain, anger, and resentment towards my parents. It's a struggle to this day, for me to remain in relationship with them. But still, I love them dearly, I appreciate them immensely, and I honor them as my parents. I understand that parents do the best we can do with the tools that we have. I have come to accept that I will always be, to them, the impossibly broken girl, who can't get her life together. That's okay because it's not my job in life to change anyone's view of me—not even my folks. I have also come to accept that my relationship, specifically with my mom, will not be what I had hoped it would be. Sometimes, life is not what we dream up in our minds and hearts, but life is always what it needs to be. Let me explain. There was a huge part of my life where my mom was my crutch; she was there for us financially for decades, she was there for us physically, she did all she knew how to do to support us in this turbulent life we found ourselves in. My mom and I would grow apart over the years—she didn't understand or accept me, and I didn't understand or accept her. It was terribly sad, it caused a lot of arguing and disconnect. I had developed, post-divorce, a coping skill that was pretty maladaptive: I would just shut you out. I didn't apply this coping skill to everyone, but I most certainly engaged this with my mom. For the purposes of understanding who Joy is and how we need to accept and face our realities, there are parts of my relationship with my mom that are significant. I can only say what I perceive and believe to be true of my mom and our relationship. For a long time, I felt bad for my mom. I felt like she got kind of a raw deal in life. Here she was: a successful woman with two totally disastrous daughters. As an adult, I can see that she probably did feel like on some level that she must have failed because her children were not, to her definition, successful or accomplished. My mother raised my niece for most of her life, but officially as a legal guardian since about 2006. That itself is a long story, however the relevance here is Samantha (my niece) was my mom's do over. My mom was going to do anything she could to ensure that Samantha would become the person, the daughter, that she could finally be proud of. I watched her mother Samantha in a way that she was incapable of mothering me; that kind of stuff messes with a person. It added to my anger, it added to my resentment, it added to my overall disdain for all things family. Most of all it hurt, solidifying the belief that I had accepted all my life: you just aren't worth enough. Like I said before, life happens exactly how it was written to happen. This too would become a piece of my story that would ultimately strengthen my voice. My mom and I might never have a relationship of mutual respect, but I will always love my mother.

Every relationship in life requires the same few basic ingredients in order for it to be successful: respect, honesty, communication, and patience. As a child, I was never shown healthy relationships; that shaped how I engaged in relationships over the course of my life. It

- Joy M. England -

took me a long time to realize that you don't need to be defensive all the time, and you don't need to pretend to be someone or something you aren't in order for people to want to befriend or choose you. As I matured and was exposed to some healthy relationships, my eyes began to open to what a true relationship means. I work daily to ensure that I engage in my relationships, whether they be close or acquaintances. Applying this newer way of interacting and thinking towards my parental relationship hasn't been as easy. For me, my relationship with my parents is difficult relationship to have, maintain, and embrace. I pray that God is able to give me the wisdom, forgiveness, and desire to be authentic and loving in my relationship with my parents. At the end of the day, no matter what has or has not happened, they are my parents, and I love them and honor them as such.

2
I Am An Adult

Hard times can seem like they follow you at times. My life, looking back, did appear to be one tragedy after another. Chaos seemed to engulf my every moment. Chaos was all that I knew, so of course it is what consumed my day to day. Years of surviving the storms is how I would describe my adult years, from nineteen to thirty-nine. At the age of eighteen I found myself, as most eighteen-year-olds do, with some newfound freedom, a sense of self-authority, and absolutely no idea how truly clueless I was. I was a community college freshman, which I honestly felt cool with, even though I had this burning hope that I would have been brave enough to chase a crazy dream of attending UCLA after graduating high school. At eighteen, I did not have the tools of self-advocacy or faith to push me; I also know now, that I was just where I was supposed to be. I started my very first full-time job at a party rental store, and let me tell you, did I think I was the coolest chick in town. This place would become a huge red marker on my path of life. This would be where I met my husband and the father of my three wonderful children.

— I Am Joy —

The party store years were a mix of good and bad, as most life stops are. It was 1996/1997, the era of beepers and Alanis Morissette (in my world anyway). It took about a year for my future husband and I to become what would now be called Facebook official. It was a fast and furious romance. We went from dating to living together in a matter of two months. We were inseparable, he was four years my elder, rode a motorcycle, and I just thought he was the best thing in the world. We bonded on a level that I have honestly not reached with anyone since. He was truly my best friend, my lover, and my supporter. I look back at the early years of our relationship and feel guilty, guilt for the trauma I brought to his already traumatized doorstep. The chaos of my family and the absolute mayhem that would wreck my body and mind in the beginning of our life together makes me feel sad for him and I. D came from a life where he had to make it on his own as a very young man, so he was accustomed to bills and responsibility for a decade prior to meeting my irresponsible self. I had no concept of money, how to keep it or how to spend it: a theme which would follow me, and still does occasionally, my entire adult life. In the beginning, D showed me how to mature. He showed me that you had to have a good work ethic, you had to be responsible for yourself and your crappy choices when they happened. He showed me that being kind mattered and that being your own person was inevitable. I was attending Kean University (College) at that time. D was proud of me, I knew he was. That was the first time I had ever remembered anyone feeling or showing pride towards me. I adored it, and I wanted more and more of it. Things were going well, really well. We lived in a cute apartment, I went to school full time and he worked full time; life was good and peaceful. No more living behind locked doors, no more worrying what I would walk into when I came home; peace felt nice. D proposed to me about six months in to our relationship, and I thought to myself, "Finally, my happy ending, my light in the darkness that has been most of my life." As many times before, Joy was always accompanied by trauma—this time in my life would be no different. My world turned upside down, seemingly overnight.

On the cusp of my twentieth birthday, I started feeling unlike myself. I couldn't verbalize it at the time, I just knew something wasn't right. Physically my body was changing; I was gaining weight, which was a trauma itself that my mind could not handle. Coupled with my physical changes came the emotional changes. It seemed overnight. I was no longer able to function. I could not get out of bed, I couldn't focus, I couldn't stop crying; I was in physical pain I couldn't understand; it felt like my body and mind were closing in on themselves. Within six months from the time I started getting sick, I had lost all control. I had gained sixty-five pounds in the first thirty days, my periods stopped, my body hurt, and my mind was so depressed and anxious it was consuming me. How could I have become a starkly different person in just six months' time? I would not know the answer to that question for twenty years. I dropped out of college and took up permanent residency on my couch. Multiple hospitals visits, doctor visits with no resolve; no one seemed to know what was happening. I was disappearing from my world. D was always there, he remained by my side, he never left, no matter how ugly it got. He showed me that you stick around when you love someone, you stay by them when they need you, you do the right thing. Little did we know then, that he was on the precipice of his own nightmare. There was no doctor who could figure out what was wrong. In 1999, a doctor said, "I think you have Polycystic Ovary Syndrome (PCOS)." Back then no one knew what that was, it had no airtime on any talk shows, there was no Web MD that could tell you all the terrifying facts. What I knew was there was this hormonal monster growing inside me, and there was also no cure. In the following years,

- I Am Joy -

I would develop Type 2 diabetes, high everything bad and low everything good. I was miserable, and I was sick beyond what I even could imagine at the time. Just when things seemed to have plummeted to the point where they couldn't get any worse, they did just that. At this point in our journey, D was working still. He was the main breadwinner for years in the beginning because I was to mentally incapable of fighting past my body shame and depression to work. We were living with friends and decided that we were going to buy a house and start to set down some roots, in hopes that it would ease the pain of our lives. We were looking forward to and actively planning our wedding. I was desperately hoping to be a mother and thought this would finally be the right step for us. A way to regain some sense of normalcy. We found a lovely little house in Long Branch (this town would become significant in later years) we just loved it and could see our lives taking root there. So, we did what everyone does: we went for a mortgage. Well, the phone rings and the mortgage woman says, "Hey Joy, there are some unpaid debts on your credit report. Do you know what these are? She reads me a list of accounts that I had no knowledge of. Remember, this was a time long before Credit Karma and 800 commercials or we-can-fix-your-credit.coms. Identity theft was not a topic on the news; it just wasn't a time of awareness for these types of crimes. I go on to ask the woman, "Well what are the addresses on these accounts because these are definitely not mine." As she reads me the mailing address, my heart sinks. What little grip I had on my identity was ripped away in that moment. The address was one I knew well—it was my sisters. Long traumatic story short, she had opened many credit cards in my name and racked up debt and never paid a penny. I was devastated, inconsolable would be the best way to describe it. I immediately called my father to report the news. Calling mom and dad was my go to reaction when anything happened with my sister. Well my dad, being exhausted from the multiple traumas at the hands of my sister, was unmoved. I felt unsupported and so deeply hurt that he couldn't understand the intensity of this moment for me. As I write this, I can tell you where I was standing in the house when I took this call and made the call to my parents. This was a life changing moment for me. In the grand scheme of my sister's actions, this was a small thing. But to me in that moment, this was everything. She had literally stolen who I was, something she tried to do on every level my entire life. It's a feeling like your biggest villain, the one your nightmares are made of, just got you. Lights out world, she won. RIP Joy. In many ways I did die in that moment. It may sound melodramatic, but losing what little bit of the identity you have at a time where you are disappearing from your own life is a game changer. I accepted defeat. I shut down. I didn't know how to fight this. I called my mom and she was angry. She was my defender. I knew she would at least fight this on my behalf. We called a family meeting. At this point my dad was living in Florida; my mom was here in NJ with my sister and me. My mom was the primary caretaker for my niece Samantha, who was almost 4 at this time. The meeting went as most did: denial, screaming, and storming out. No resolution, no answers. Just more anger and chaos. I was used to no resolution. When you grow up with a sister who steals and lies constantly, no resolution becomes the norm. There was no remedy. I was left so broken it would take decades to assemble the pieces.

In the wake of the drama with my sister, D and I took my dad up on an offer and moved to Florida, in hopes of a fresh start. D worked; he always was employed, and I was not. I was barely functioning, so the weight of the finances and everything was on him. D had been battling his own demons for some time at this point, which I was unaware of, in part because he hid it and part because I was so self-absorbed

- I Am Joy -

I couldn't have seen it if he wore it as a shirt. Florida wasn't good. Florida would be where D and I were married. Florida would be where D would attempt to take his life for the first time. Florida was dark, D was dark. Things changed in Florida and they would never, ever return to what they were before. D and I were married in 1999, and I think we both hoped that this would be the new start that we prayed for. The years following Florida, and before the birth of our first son, were filled with moves from house to house and state to state. We would ultimately end up back in NJ. My health got so bad that my mom thought (she was right) that my best care would be in NJ. D was left out; he wasn't given the support he needed. I failed him; in my darkness I just couldn't give him what he needed. I couldn't be there for him as he was for me, and I will always feel sorry for that. Over the next few years, D would spiral into places that nightmares are made of. Things went from bad to Lifetime Movie bad. Despite this, we had some bright spots, and I THANK GOD for them every day.

Upon return to NJ, I was diagnosed with Type 2 Diabetes. I was very overweight, miserable, and wishing I would just disappear. Married life felt the same as non-married life did: sad with moments of happiness. My family was growing tired of my ailments and issues; but D always stood by me, ER visit after ER visit, he was there. I remember distinctly feeling so grateful to him for being what I had never had; someone who believed in me. I could not see at the time that I was becoming a believer in myself as well. I was embattled in my first journey of advocacy: saving myself.

D was changing; he was morphing into someone who I would come to know as a monster. Depression was eating him alive, and I was too sick, too selfish, and to sad to notice the changes. Married life was hard, lonely, and all around something that felt extraordinarily anticlimactic. April of 2000, I found out I was expecting my first baby. You would think this would be a joyous occasion. D and I were thrilled—everyone else, and I mean everyone else not so much. More on this in a future chapter.

After the birth of my first son in December of 2000, married life would become even harder, and not for the reasons that would make sense. D and I continued growing apart; we had lost the connection that we used to feel. All I can gather is between his mental health struggles and my all-consuming medical issues we just lost the energy to put into our relationship. For D, our marital disconnect manifested in him seeking attention and solace outside of the marriage. D would go on to cheat for the remainder of our nine years of marriage. Over the course of our marriage, we would endure countless financial disasters, ongoing family traumas at the hands of my sister, job loss, evictions, hunger, and poverty. D was ravished with Bipolar Disorder and that caused not only the sexual deviance, but also robbed him of his ability to hold down a job. I would become a part of the workforce in 2001 and would remain the consistently employed adult in the house. D and I never got to enjoy marriage. We were both in personal prisons of pain and trauma that stole any joy from our lives. D turned to infidelity to ease his pain. I turned to food and spending to ease mine. I would go on to endure and tolerate nine years of his cheating and lying; the "others" included a few best friends (I use that term lightly) and many more strangers. I hated him for it, I hated me for it, I hated the women for it; hate and rage became my norm. In spite of the pain and the constant emotional abuse. We would remain legally married for twelve years, separated three of those years. I hated myself for staying more than I hated him for the emotional abuse.

The cheating was never really hidden well. I felt so horrible about myself that even though it ripped me apart, we would scream and fight about it. He would deny and lie to my face. I stayed; I accepted it as my lot in life. Many women stay, for their own reasons, but they stay. I know now that for me, I needed to stay. I needed to experience the intolerable emotional abuse, because it would later become the very thing that gave me back my voice.

    The first affair that I was aware of, involved my "best friend" and started when my son was about six months old. This affair would go on to last over a year. All the while D would be angry with me for not treating her nicely, because even though I couldn't prove it, I knew they were sleeping together. Women always know. The apex of this affair would be when I would return home from work one evening, approximately seven months pregnant with my second son, to the both of them in my living room, telling me that they were in love and that they were going to raise my children together. Something happened to me in that moment, as my "best friend" sat in my living room, on my couch, telling me that I am no longer welcome in my home and that she and my husband were going to take my kids. I remember this moment in time so clearly. I believe we all have these moments, both good and bad, that are imprinted so vibrantly in our minds that there is no way we can forget them. My husband's girlfriend, my friend, looked me in the eyes and said that she was going to mother my son and take my unborn son when he was born as well. The hell she was. I remember looking at D and seeing a look on his face that I will never forget, not a look of shame or regret, but a look of calmness, almost like he was relieved that he could stop hiding; I think that moment hurt more than the admission of the physical affair. I knew right then, unequivocally, that D was no longer my person. He was the enemy, and I would hold onto that description of him forever more. The end result was that I was not leaving my home and they were not going to take my boys. They left, together and I was left alone, more broken than I thought possible. Even though I was unable to deny what I had already known to be true of D, that he was lying and cheating, I stayed with him, a decision that would bring shame to me for years. It was also a decision that would engage a seed of advocacy that was buried so deeply inside me. A seed that would manifest into a voice for women's ability to be who they need to be, alone or in a relationship. Staying in a marriage after such trauma and pain is pure misery. For the person who gets cheated on, your world becomes, checking, double checking, tracking, questioning, suspecting, and total and complete unrest. It was miserable; it wasn't a life, it was an existence. Little did I know that I was developing a definition of marriage and relationship that was quite twisted and dark. I had been operating in a state of survival mode for my entire life—married life was no different. Living with D was torture. He was so angry, so cruel, so mean; I didn't know at the time that depression could cause all of this. In survival mode you do what you need to in the moment—you don't think about the future or the consequences long term. You think about right here, right now. I had a little boy who needed me, one already living in this world of darkness and one growing inside me; I vowed to protect them at all costs. The remainder of my married life would become me against D, me against the darkness of that marriage, me making a way to stop surviving and start living. I didn't know it at the time, but I was on the precipice of one of the two darkest days of my life.

Easter Sunday 2003. As a Christian today, I know the significance of Easter, the absolute miracle of the Third Day. In 2003, however, I was clueless. The day started as most did at that time: sad and terrifying. As I prepared my son for the day at his grandmother's, D was angry...angrier than usual. He didn't want to come with us to my mom's, and I wanted him to. In an attempt to keep up the facade that everything was okay. He eventually got in the car to come with us and grew increasingly angrier. I don't remember why, but I turned

- I Am Joy -

the car around and brought him back home. He got out of the car with a slam and stormed to the house. I remember watching him for a minute, and he went over to his car retrieved something from the trunk and went back to the house. I knew something was brewing, I just had no idea what it was. As my son and I returned home that day, I knew in my gut something was wrong. I pulled up to the house, my son sleeping peacefully in the back seat. I went to the door, our typically barky dog laid quiet just staring at me. As I walked toward our bedroom, I saw the glow of the TV under the door. It was like an out of body experience; I was watching myself approach the door. I opened the door to find D collapsed on the bed. I immediately called 911. As the operator tried to tell me what to do for D, I just kept screaming my baby is in the car. I couldn't help D. They told me to prop him up, find out what he took. I couldn't move, I couldn't function. Eventually I would retrieve a bottle of Tylenol PM from the floor, a huge Costco sized bottle. I propped D up at the insistence of the 911 operator, and I left the room. I went to the car to get my son. I was sobbing, screaming, it was a terror like none I had ever felt before. The police arrived, and we stood in the kitchen. I was covering my son's eyes as they dragged D's lifeless body from the bedroom to the stretcher. I wish I could tell you now that the rest was a blur, but it isn't. I remember every moment, every smell, every feeling, every tear. It is something that will never leave me. My kind neighbor agreed to drive my son and I to the hospital. As we were in the car, my two-year-old grabs my hand and says, "It will be okay, Mommy". My two-year-old hero. The treatment for someone who has just ingested three hundred Tylenol PM tablets was intense and horrible: stomach pumping, judgmental medical staff, shots, scans, bloodwork—it was endless. As I stood beside my husband, curtain drawn, all I see are my baby's two little feet dangling off the chair as he sits there eating his graham crackers and apple juice. As the male nurse struggles to get D to comply with the stomach pump hose, D turns and yanks the hose, causing the charcoal to splatter all over me. This was probably one of, if not the lowest points of my life. Talk about feeling helpless. I stood there trying to clean myself up as best I can, then D sits up puts his hand on my belly and asks for Pam. The nurse says, "Are you Pam?" I said, "No, that would be his girlfriend, my best friend." Not knowing what to do, the nurse walks out. There I stand, seven months pregnant, splattered with charcoal from my suicidal cheating husband; defeated would be an understatement. My mom arrives and takes my son with her, and I eventually go home. D would remain in the hospital ICU for a week, and then two weeks in a behavioral health hospital. Life didn't get much easier; nothing really changed for me or my marriage; we just kept on surviving.

Living with the reality of what my life had become was more than my mind and spirit could handle. I was an unemployed, pregnant, mother of a toddler. My husband was for all intent and purposes my enemy. I am not sure how one deals with all of that at once. My coping skill was to push it down, keep focused on right now. Right now I needed to make sure my unborn son had what he needed, and that my toddler was as unaffected as possible. Since D was no longer working, I had moved into my mother's home for the duration of my pregnancy; this was anything but ideal. It was hard on so many levels. For the majority of my life I either felt ignored or shamed; at this point in my life, it was the latter. D moved with my father, who was now living in Virginia, so my dad could keep an eye on him and help him get work. Owen and I didn't see much of D the remainder of my pregnancy; he was either too tired or too self-absorbed to make the trip to NJ. Back then, recovery of significant mental health was an extremely ineffective model. D became a person I did not recognize: he was self-centered to the point of total narcissism—everything was about him and how he was recovering. Don't get me wrong, he needed to heal and get better. I understood that, but we also needed him to be a father and husband; he was incapable of that. I was angry, really angry, the kind of angry that I now know will eat you alive. What I didn't realize in those moments was that God was working. He was setting the stage for the comeback of my wildest dreams. It took a long time, over a decade to be exact, but great works take time. Alongside my anger lived a deep sorrow. I was mourning. Mourning the life I thought I would have had, mourning the man I thought I knew as my husband, most of all I was mourning the Joy I thought I would never become. I was surrounded by judgement and ridicule: both internal and external. Sadly, this was just the beginning of the chaos and tragedy that would run through my life. It has become part of my life's work to heal that little girl in her communion dress and honor the woman who would go on to face immeasurable sadness and grief.

I felt immense shame in my life. From a very young age, I learned to be ashamed. I was unaware that feeling ashamed was not how everyone felt. Everyone at some point in their life feels ashamed of a decision or action or event in their life. It is a part of the human experience. When I describe being ashamed, I implore you to understand the force of the shame in my life. The shame was not fleeting. It was never healed, it was never diminished. It grew and grew; it was all I knew. It was so consuming that I stopped searching for redeeming qualities in myself. I accepted the innate deficits that I believed were the only labels I would ever have. It is a sad day when you accept the false belief that you are not capable of anything positive at the tender age of ten. One thing about acceptance is that it initiates some relief. The relief for me when I accepted my labels of shame was the relief from having to figure it out. I stopped trying to figure out why I was ashamed; I just accepted that I was shameful. That label of shame would be the label that was most prominent. I walked into a room with shame first; it led the way, it ordered my steps, it decided what I would allow and what I deserved. It was shame that put me in positions of harm. It was shame that stunted my evolution in this wonderful kingdom. As evil as my shame was, it was also my best friend, my confidant, my protector, and my advisor. Like many other dark things in my life, I wanted the darkness to accept me. I wanted to be loved so desperately that I would seek love from the very things that were destroying me. I wish I could say that there was a giant AH HA moment where I stood up and removed the label in an amazing show of strength and courage. There was no AH HA, there was no huge display... What there was, was this still small voice buried so deep under the layers of labels that kept saying, "Keep going Joy, keep moving, find the strength to believe in yourself. It was that still small voice that produced, over time, the belief that I could do it. I could accomplish the things of my heart's desires. Over time, little by little, those beliefs would get bigger and bigger. They still took a backseat to my prominent labels, but they were moving into focus now. I could see there was more to who Joy was than just shame and failure. There were specks of brightness.. Those specks of light were breaking through the cracks in the armor of shame that encapsulated me. Cracks in the belief system I had known my entire life. Over the course of a decade, these cracks grew to the point that illumination began to overtake the darkness. A light that I never knew existed. The acceptance that I had the power to remove those expired labels and pick up the labels of LOVED, REDEEMED, FORGIVEN, WORTHY, BEAUTIFUL, SMART, ACCOMPLISHED, UNDERSTOOD, SURVIVOR, LEADER, MOTHER, AUNT, FRIEND, and the most important label of them all: SAVED. Salvation is the ultimate source of light. There is nothing to dark for salvation to enlighten.

'Declare with your mouth and believe in your heart that Jesus is Lord and God raised him from the dead, you will be saved' (Romans 10:9).

- Joy M. England -

I AM A MOTHER

MOTHERHOOD WAS SOMETHING that I had always thought would happen for me. I, as many women, had no idea just how life changing motherhood is. Earlier I touched on the trauma that surrounded my pregnancies. The details surrounding my entrance to motherhood is worth some additional noting. I was really physically sick when I got pregnant with my eldest son, Owen. D and I were also in no financial position to be bringing in a baby, so needless to say, few were happy for us. Even now, seventeen years later, I can vividly remember the shame that consumed me the entirety of my pregnancy. Once again, my old best friend shame was tagging along with me. There were some really great parts to my pregnancy with Owen. D and I grew closer, and we worked tirelessly on his carousel nursery. D hand painted a life size carousel horse on the wall; it was breathtaking. As any first-time mother, I was full of wonder and anxiety for what Owen would be like. Along with the curiosity of how my baby would be, I also hoped for the chance to celebrate my miracle baby boy. As life would have it, celebration wasn't in the cards for my pregnancy. D and I did our best to be all the celebration we needed, however it was inevitable to not feel hurt when everyone you love can't love you enough to be there for you.

By the grace of God, I welcomed a beautiful baby boy into this world on December 5, 2000. I was elated and in awe of this miracle that was all mine. Motherhood was something that took a bit of time for me to find my stride; your entire life changes in an instant, so catching up is an interesting event. I loved being a mom, even though I was exhausted, confused, and worried, ninety percent of the time I still loved being who Owen needed me to be. God blessed me another miracle pregnancy in 2002/2003. I had hoped that this pregnancy might have been met with a little better reception since I felt I had "proven" myself a worthy mom over the past two years. Unfortunately, this pregnancy was met with the same reception as Owen's: discontent and borderline anger. I really could never understand why people were so unhappy at the thought of me becoming a mother. My thinking then was the flaw must be something in me; I have since learned the flaw was not mine, it was theirs. To set the stage for my second pregnancy, things were strained in the family, which wasn't something new. My sister and her husband were divorced, or divorcing, which meant my nieces were living separately. My eldest niece was living in between my sister's home and my mother's home. My youngest niece was living between my sister's home and her biological father's home. The family was disjointed. As many times before, everyone was in survival mode, living in a constant state of fear about what my sister would do next. D and I were not in a great spot; his demons were raging inside of him, and I was trying as hard as I could to ignore the life that I was trapped in. Owen and this pregnancy were the only bright spots that kept me feeling somewhat encouraged. Announcing my pregnancy to the family happened on Christmas Eve. Christmas Eve at that time meant a gathering of friends and family at my mother's home for food, laughs, and present exchanges. This particular Christmas Eve, the "best friend" I mentioned was also in attendance (at this point, the confession of the affair had not been made). During the present exchange, Owen asked my mom to help him open his present, which was a hand painted T-shirt, that said I AM Going To Be A Big Brother. The revelation was met with utter silence. The jubilation and excitement that I had hoped for did not occur. There were a few congratulations, and then the room just moved on to the next present exchange. I wasn't surprised; I was hurt in a way that I don't know if you ever really recover from, but we put smiles on our faces and continued the gift exchange. To this day, I cannot explain or rationalize why I was treated that way. I don't understand why people who are supposed to love you can be so horrible. What I do know is that was their issue and not mine, no matter how hard they wanted me to believe I was shameful and unworthy. I remember with my first pregnancy, when D and I were visiting my dad, we were at the table talking and the topic of D's and I wedding came up and I said, just as a side bar, that I had forgotten the something blue on my wedding day and that I hoped that wasn't bad luck. My dad's response was, "Well maybe that's why you are pregnant now." I was stunned to the core for my dad, who never had much to say about anything, to feel so strongly that my pregnancy was a bad thing. I didn't know what to do other than to shut all the way down. I never spoke another word about my pregnancy to my dad. It was things like this that reinforced the internal belief that I was tragically flawed. Regardless of whether or not my family and friends were excited, I was happy. I knew in my heart that I was meant to be a mother. Deep down inside me, it was these moments that ignited my internal battle cry; I didn't understand then but these moments were creating the warrior that I would become.

Samantha Marie

Long before I physically knew motherhood, I was blessed to experience aunt-hood. Where do I start with the little girl who brought a family together? I was the first person to hold you. I couldn't believe how much I loved you instantly. You put smiles on the faces of a family that had known decades of sorrow. You were and always will be an inspiration. You had it tough; you had so many unanswered pieces of your life. I couldn't understand because of the pain that had swallowed me whole that you were hurting, that you needed me in a way

— I Am Joy —

I could not provide you. That reality is something I confront daily to ensure I remain in a place of forgiving myslef for having failed you. In spite of the selfish and self-centered adults in your life, you embraced life. You were truly the definition of an advocate for yourself. As you grew, we grew to be more like sisters than aunt and niece. The bond we share is something that time, mistakes, anger, and hurt can't begin to tarnish. You have grown into a woman who I admire. You are a woman who is a testament to perseverance and grace. Our relationship has changed in intensity and frequency over the years, and many times I feared it would be lost. I know now that times change, relationships shift, but that love never leaves. I hope I have shown you good things in your life. I hope I have made you proud. You have made me immensely proud, not only due to your accomplishments but because of the person and woman that you are. I love you like you are my daughter, I admire you like you are my best friend, and I cherish you like a sister. Thank you for your love and relationship over the years. Keep making history.

OWEN, MY WARRIOR

DECEMBER 5, 2000 was a day that changed me forever. I was a mother, holy crap! A mother, I had dreamed of this moment, and fought for this moment, and I had accomplished in doing something great for the first time in a very long time. Owen, meaning young warrior, was born. You were and are perfect. Just a dreamboat. I never loved anything or anyone the way I loved you from the moment you were born. How could such a perfect, beautiful being be birthed from me, someone so full of pain and chaos and disease? I didn't know God at this time in my life, but boy did God know me. Owen, you were a gift on immeasurable levels. You became my drive and strength. You would grow into the meaning of your name in ways I could never imagine. You were born into the chaotic world we had come to claim as normal. I truly believed I had no choice other than to accept chaos and sorrow. Then you was born and showed me that I could choose Joy. The love that D and I had for you was magical. We adored you and celebrated every move you made. It was total bliss. I still had my many issues, and weight problems, and self-esteem issues, but I was able to function more. I worked nights and D worked days; we seemed to finally be working towards the independence that we hadn't ever been able to grasp.

Owen, you were perfect, and you were our first born, and first boy, and so therefore you were spoiled. You were my best friend, and albeit that was probably not healthy, it was the truth. You were my everything. D and I had lost any remnants of what we once were. I had lost all trust and faith in him, and I imagine he felt the same about me. I focused on you, Owen. Were you happy? Were you healthy? Were you cared for? That was all that mattered.

You grew and became this spunky little man. My awe of you never dimmed. You have the type of personality that draws everyone in. Of course, you are not without your struggles in life. The spirit of rejection and abandonment is generational. But you have the strength and the courage to end this generational curse. Your bravery is one I have never seen in my life; it's just one of your gifts from God. If someone is lucky enough for you to love them, then they have experienced loyalty and love unmatched by any other.

Nathanial James, my gift from God

Where to begin! The gift from God that I knew I wanted and could not have known how much I would have needed. We call this gift Nate. I don't think you realize the incredible human being that you are. I know I am the parent, but you have taught me so much over your short fourteen years. I have learned in great part how to forgive by watching your example, specifically teaching me the most important thing about forgiveness: forgiving yourself. You came into this world during a time of hurt, pain, transition, trauma, and utter confusion. Your presence alone changed the reality that Owen and I had become way too comfortable in. You were an easy baby; you just loved to be loved and Owen adored his baby brother from the moment he knew you were here.

    You were my summer baby, my bright light in a dimming world. You were perfect in every way and we all just rallied around this beautiful blessing. Even though there was no excitement around my pregnancies, my family loved the babies. You were such a pleasure to take care of. Owen and I just ate up every second of your entrance into our lives. Life hasn't always been fair or easy but you have a heart that can make anyone forget that the times are bad and cause you to remember that there is a blessing in every moment. Nate, you are my partner in crime; we were inseparable for years. It has been an honor to watch you develop into a young man capable of doing anything you set your mind too. I am so grateful to God for the blessing that is my Nathanial James.

I AM MOVING ON

LIFE HAS A funny way of not waiting for anyone. I thank God every day for the power that was always in me to keep pushing, to keep going even when all I wanted to do was disappear. I didn't know it was there, but I had the beginnings of belief in myself. I knew there was greater out there for me. I knew I was capable of more than my life to date had told me I was. I started back at college when I was pregnant

— *Joy M. England* —

with my first son, and I would remain chasing my education dreams for the next eleven years. I would finally obtain a BS degree in 2011. Through those eleven years, I gave birth to my two sons, carried and lost a daughter, and got divorced. My Faith Warrior-ness was in full effect, although it felt very similar to loss and failure. Your destiny is your destiny—it is already written. My call would turn out to be one that even my wildest dreams could not have imagined. We may not know how we keep going, but what matters is that we do.

In 2008, I find myself a single mother signing the lease to a one-bedroom apartment. In that moment, I felt like a failure, but in reality it was the beginning of my comeback. My boys and I would go on to live in that one-bedroom apartment for four years, creating some of the best memories of our lives. I was trying to assemble the pieces of my life. Who was I now? Who would I become? How do I navigate this post marriage world? I was still angry, like a burning rage type of anger. I was still very physically sick, and in denial about just how bad it was. I felt alone, I felt disappointed in myself, I felt desperate. My inner talk became some of the most hateful things that one could imagine. So here I am, with two young boys watching me. What do I do now? Well to say I made mistakes would be grossly understated—I made huge mistakes. My anger was in the driver seat, which is never a good thing. Even in the fury of rage and despair, I made a solid decision: therapy. This would become a piece of what saved us all, not just for me, but for my beautiful boys who were adjusting to this new world too.

Therapy is hard work. I found myself in a love/hate relationship with the process of healing and closure. We would spend years in the therapy office a few times per week. We didn't know it at the time, but we were learning the skills we desperately needed to recover and move forward. No matter how hard I had tried to keep my boys safe when I was married, I didn't always succeed. I grew up always feeling

– I Am Joy –

unsafe. So inside of me, totally subconsciously, I vowed to never allow my children to live in an unsafe home. The hard truth is for years we did live in an unsafe home; however, our new apartment was peaceful. It was safe; there were no surprises lurking around the corner. That was a gift that we all three would come to appreciate greatly. Therapy taught me so much about life, myself, and acceptance. I struggled with the Joy I thought that I would be versus the Joy who was walking in this new life. I still attend therapy at the same center that saved me and my boys all those years ago. I can't find a big enough word to describe the gratitude I have towards the New Jersey Center for the Healing Arts. Thank you for showing us what love and healing look like and, most importantly, what they feel like.

We hear the term moving on so much in our world that it really has become diluted. Moving on takes patience and kindness towards yourself; it also takes a whole lot of bravery. Moving on for the most part is empowering, once you can heal past the pain and the anger. I have had to move past so many things in my life, really big and painful things; but I survived I am here to tell the tale. You can move on too. You can be at peace with your life while hoping for your bright future. Honoring where you come from, no matter how dark or traumatic is the most important factor of moving on. For years I thought that moving on only pertained to leaving a romantic relationship. Moving on can, and does, take on a million shapes. For me, moving on from being a victim was my biggest. At times in my life I certainly felt like a victim. I would tell anyone who would stand still long enough of the travesties that I had endured. The constant sharing of my pain was not to gain sympathy; it was my attempt, albeit feeble, to ease the pain I was in. I thought if I could get some solidarity or validation from someone about the pain I was in then maybe it would ease. That's not how moving on works—the fix or the solve can't ever come from another person. Just like it was you who endured and survived

— Joy M. England —

it, it must be you who mourns it and heals it. Moving on takes a great deal of intentional effort to honor your history, feel the pain, forgive everyone (including yourself) and letting go. Truly letting go of the power the pain had over you seems impossible when you are engulfed by it, but I stand here as a testimony that it can be done. There were so many things and people in my world that I needed to move on from that it felt like I would be left all alone. The hard truth is that sometimes God will bring you down to no one so you will look up to find the only one. For a long time, I really didn't have anyone in the natural world who could be there for me. Not because every person I ever met sucked, but because my brokenness required attention, and that attention can't happen if you are fixing your eyes on distractions. What felt like more and more loss was really just a set up to succeed at moving on. Once I embraced the process of moving on, which meant that I had to let go not only of the what happened to me-isms, I had to let go of me. Before we move on from whatever we need to move on from, we need to understand where and how those things took root (which in some cases might be appropriate and healthy). In my situation it was anything but. I had grown so used to trauma and sadness that I didn't know how to define myself if I wasn't surviving something. If we boil the notion of moving on down to its purest form, I believe what you find is pretty simple: permission. Permission to be free from whatever it was that kept you bound. Permission to leave that older version of you in the past. Permission to say I forgive you, but I am not going to remain here any longer. Most importantly, it is permission to redefine who you are.

3
What If

What if I was stronger? What if I was wiser? What if I was richer? What if I was thinner? What if I was younger? What if I was better? What If I was not the person I am today? What if I had not been brave enough to keep going? What IF my story was different? What if it's a question we all ask; it's one that I have wrestled with for decades. The answer I learned was this: my what ifs constructed my I AMs and for that I am immeasurably thankful.

    We all ask ourselves at some point in our lives, "What if?". What if we had done this or that? What if we had dated or not dated so and so? Well I am no different. My life is littered with what ifs; at times, these what ifs became all-consuming regrets. My relationship with God has taught me that all things are planned, and even when we elect to use our free will, He already knew what we would choose. It all becomes part of the foundation of who we are eventually destined to become. This revelation took years of healing, prayer, therapy, and maturity getting to a point where I could love and honor my what ifs so that I always remember their purpose. Life takes a million twists and turns, resulting in a million what ifs. Here are some of my highlights.

Wondering and allowing myself to live in an imaginary world of what if quite frankly saved me from losing my mind as a kid. All kids imagine and wonder what life would be if they were this or that, or if they lived here or there. For me, I think I lived in a world that felt so alternate from what I saw life to be through watching other people. That contrast is what allowed my imagination to focus on the what ifs of my future; that kept me sane. A distinct what if when I was younger was what if I had a big family. I dreamed of brothers and sisters to protect me and care for me. As I grew, that dream turned from siblings to marrying into a family where there were a lot of siblings and finding my family that way. I held onto that what if for a long time. Then I married a man with one brother and a family in an equal level of discord to my family. God has a funny way of keeping us from what we think we need right then, to show us exactly what we needed we had all along. I still hold out hope for marrying into a large family. I think I am ready now; I have done the work to heal myself from my past. I can embrace a large family and not feel like the voice that was never heard. I had to do a lot of work within myself to heal from the hurt of my family of origin. No matter what my angry teenage years will tell you, the anger I felt towards my family and extended family came from my deep sadness that I didn't have them in my life. I love my family. I pray for my family daily, I hope that they have lived lives rich in love and laughter. I have faith that God removed them for a reason and will bring them back in His timing.

Love is hard, love is tough, and love has always been a Goliath what if. Being in a troubled relationship for my entire adult life, I was ill prepared at best for the world of dating. Not only was I insecure to the point of almost being a total recluse, I was also really like an eigh-

Joy M. England

teen-year-old with no social skills as it related to the opposite sex. I remained single for about four years after my divorce. I would love to say it was by choice, but it was by happenstance. I wanted a relationship. I wanted to be a part of a couple, I just had a very rose-colored glasses view of what that would be. I wasn't in a place to acknowledge my role in my marriage or to acknowledge the amount of deep pain I was still in. I just wanted to move on, whatever that meant. I knew I wanted more babies and a happy marriage. I was still so scared to think of what life would be like for me and the boys if we were to navigate it with only me at the helm. To add to the confusion of singleness, I was finally on the verge of accomplishing what had been one of my longest running goals in life: graduation! It had taken me so long, through so much heartache, but I had done it! I graduated Rutgers University and felt pride for the first time since becoming a mom. So here I was, scared, confused, vulnerable, and graduated. Now what? I wasn't sure who I was if I wasn't a student. I took the GRE (Graduate Record Exam) and applied to graduate school. I was accepted into the School of Public Affairs and Administration and was embarking on a Masters in Public Administration. On top of this new endeavor, I landed my first post bachelors' job. Warrior status #Epic.

I was so excited to accept a leadership role in a program that was all new to me. It felt right. I didn't know why I received this or how important this role would be, but God was at work. So, I leapt into something that was scary and new, leapt without knowing what it would look like or mean. The courage to leap was something I came to realize is be a big part of who I am. I was in what turned out to be my element. I felt proud for the first time in a long time; I felt like I was making real changes. I was plugging along, starting graduate school and just doing my leadership thing when BAM, out of nowhere one single text changed the entire trajectory of my world. I never really believed in the starstruck love that Taylor Swift sings about, but then I experienced Mack.

Boy oh boy was I in love, the kind of love that gives you butterflies and turns you into a blubbering hot mess. It was also the kind of love that consumed me, my mind, my heart, and my actions. To this day, I do believe that this was a mutual love—at first. There are some things that you just can't fake. What I failed to realize was when the love changed, and when I changed and became someone that I hope to never meet again. Dating was fun. D and I dated, but it was a different type of dating. Mack and I, if I am honest, went on one real date, which seems ridiculous looking back, given the level of submission I sunk to with him. Mack was really good at making me feel like I was the only one, and he was even better at making me feel like I would never be good enough. We shared what had to be ten thousand text messages over the course of the three years that we "dated"; I use that term extremely loosely. We worked together, so I saw him almost daily. We would see each other at my house in the evenings or occasionally on weekends—seemed normal enough. Eventually you will wonder why we only met at my house and never his house or never out in public. The answer, my friends, is simple: he lived with the mother of his child and had countless others all over, so public was never an option. I am sure what comes to mind as you read this is why would I "date" someone who lived with another woman? Not sure if it was me being naïve, or just wanting to believe him, but he told me that they lived together for financial reasons only. I know I know, enter massive eye rolls here. One other really important fact to know about this "relationship" was that it had to be a secret. I was his boss and that was frowned upon at work. I realized years later how clever he really was. He picked someone who he knew would have to be discreet, which suited his needs impeccably. Well done Mack, well done. I digress. Here we go. Boys, you might want to skip to the next chapter here. I am going there—sex: the inevitable adult thing we do in relationships, right? What if I didn't have extreme trauma around sex from a cheating husband who blamed me for his decade-long affair? What if I was a woman who honored her body instead of shaming it? What if I was a woman who could see through the smoke screens and see the real person behind the sweet texts? I still struggle with a few of these particular what ifs because some things can't ever be undone. I would learn that the very hard way. Sex is normal. It's a human urge but unfortunately, many times we treat it like something casual; it's really anything but. Mack was my first partner since my ex-husband. He was the epitome of what I thought I wanted and what I thought I needed to escape what I had known. I quickly realized that sex was a weapon, a tool that Mack used to make himself feel better about who he was and who he was not. I would become just another pawn, something that he would pick up or put down when it suited him. I started to take on his inadequacies, as sex will do to you; Soul ties are no joke. For those of you unfamiliar with soul ties, this is a spiritual term used to describe the resulting connections left behind when you have sex with someone. A soul tie between a husband and wife is a beautiful thing. Soul ties as a result of sin and fornication are the farthest things from beautiful. Most of us go around collecting soul ties with people who we eventually learn are not good for us, let alone a beloved. As women, soul ties are particularly dangerous; we are the receivers in the equation of sex. Think about it. You don't need me to explain it, right? We receive all the soul ties of our partners. Knowing what I have shared with you about Mack and his lengthy list of partners, can you imagine the state of my soul? Horribly tragic and deeply sad. Mack was a traumatized, tortured soul. I don't think he realized how destructive he was—at least I pray that he

- I Am Joy -

didn't realize it. My relationship with Mack quickly became an emotionally abusive relationship. I surrendered all to this man who didn't deserve an ounce of me. Mack had the ability to suck you in and capture your being in a way that you would do whatever he asked of you, accepting what little pieces he would throw your way as appeasement. I loved him. I know I opened with that, but it bears repeating. I have come to learn that this type of love isn't really love; it's hate, it's pain, it's torture. This type of relationship is one I would never wish upon anyone. I am so thankful to God that I will never accept anything like this in my life again. Mack taught me that sex was what mattered, that women were meant to be subjects of pleasure and nothing more. Mack taught me that women are less than, not worthy of respect or love. Mack taught me that men can be hateful, mean, and evil. In so many ways, this relationship was a hundred times darker than my marriage ever was. As a result, I was broken in new ways that felt like they would kill me. This "relationship" became a boomerang of break ups and drama. There's something you need to understand about a shattered woman: we accept anything, especially the things that keep us shattered. I knew Mack was in relationship with countless others. I may not have confronted him with it, but I knew. We always know. I looked the other way; I chose to believe the lies that this was what I had to accept. Even when the doctor calls and says, "Joy, you have an incurable sexually transmitted disease," I still stayed. My friends, brokenness is dangerous—it's deadly. The good news is that it is also curable. Thank you, God, for the cure. I wish I could say that I woke up one day and said, "Enough! I am leaving. I deserve better." That's not at all how it ended; it ended with Mack telling me that he picked someone else and to get over it. Seems relatively kind, given his history of unkindness. It was that moment that God used to show me that I needed to save my life. The call on my life in this world was bigger than the anchor to hell and self-hate that Mack had become. When it finally ended, I can't verbalize the internal destruction that I felt. The hurt was unbearable. I was never a cutter in my life. I had times in my youth where I would injure myself to get attention, but this with Mack was not that. I couldn't hold the pain, so I hurt myself to ease it. It didn't work, it just created a physical manifestation of the emotional turmoil. I was in the pits of total darkness. There was no glimmer of light—it was all consuming. In this darkness, my spiritual mother reached her hand out to me and lead me to salvation. I was saved in the darkness of sin. I was saved when I thought I was not salvageable, let alone worthy of salvation.

I feel compelled to remind you that while I was willingly following this soul destructing path, I was still a mother, a full-time employee, and a full-time graduate student. Nothing but God carried me through the three years that I was fully bought into the Mack life. What if I had been a more present mom? What if I had focused more on my family and career? What if I hadn't been so stupid? What ifs are killers, and they officially murdered what little bit of self-esteem I had left. What if I hadn't been with Mack? Would I have found my salvation? What if I hadn't been so shattered? God wouldn't have been able to show His total restorative glory. I am so thankful for Mack. I embrace my Mack years—they were not lost years; they were learning years. Sometimes the very things we pray for are the same things that explode the idea of who we thought we were. Mack taught me immeasurably. He taught me about boundaries, about truth, about love, about relationship. Mack showed me everything that I never want to be again. What if I had not answered that text? What if I had felt better about myself? What if I had not believed the lies of the enemy telling me that this was all I deserved. The answer is I wouldn't be the woman I am today if it hadn't had been for Mack. For that Mack, I thank you.

- I Am Joy -

My experience with romantic loves, as depicted, is not vast. However, my few encounters were impactful and important. I would be remiss if I did not share with all of you the ways in which I really went left in regard to love, like, and lust. As we know, I was saved in 2014, and I was still engaging in these ungodly relationships. While chasing after my salvation. We all struggle. Strongholds are real and soul ties, as we discussed, are nothing to laugh at. Sprinkle all that with some low self-esteem and you have a perfect storm. I was hurting in ways that were so deep that I almost didn't even realize it was pain. I had accepted it as reality, and that is so dangerous. Your thinking drives your acting, and when your thinking is riddled with sin and self-hate, your actions are sure to be destructive. During the time that Mack was coming to an explosive end, I had begun speaking with a man whom I had thought for a long time was someone so far out of my league. Low and behold, he did not think so and we ended up "dating". Yup there are those quotation marks again. Yours truly had not learned a blessed thing yet. I was filling one painful void with another painful void. This time around, the man appeared on paper to be in a much more similar mindset to me: he was Masters prepared, successful, accomplished. He appeared to be really a mature person who would be a good contrast to what I was used to. Everything in me, deep down, the me who was fighting to be heard knew that he was the same as Mack just in a suit. He wasn't a God called man in my life. He was not saved and was not interested in anything other than what suited his needs and protected him from his prior hurts. The difference with him and Mack was that with him I could empathize. He had been so badly hurt by women in the past that he now saw all women as enemies. Hurt people hurt people, and that he did. It turned into what was a very toxic few years. I wanted so desperately for he and I to be "it". I tolerated so much more than anyone should. I take responsibility for some of the toleration because it was due to my deep hurt, low self-worth, and ignoring God telling me to walk away. There was yelling and degrading, torment and disappearance. There was confusion and manipulation, and that should not ever be in a relationship between two people. I think back to a few moments that really stuck out to me, now that I have healed and forgiven myself and him. I remember asking him if he loved me, via text, because he rarely (if ever) answered the phone. He responded a day later with, "No Joy, I don't love you," followed by a text that said, "You upset?" I was crushed, devastated, and then I remained in the relationship another year. It's heartbreaking what we will accept when we don't accept Jesus first. The fleshly side of me would love to say that I dislike him, but I don't. I forgive him, and I pray that he finds the healing he needs. I endured years of relationships that taught me that sex was all I was worth. I spent a total of five years with men who never put in any effort, never took me on a date, never tried to get to know me. Men who were utterly unavailable in every conceivable way. God needed to have me experience them and then remove them, so He could show me in my isolation that that the worth I should be chasing is my own.

I AM A FRIEND

FRIENDSHIP IS NOT only important, it's also an inevitable experience in life. Some of us experience friendship or experience the absence of friendship. I imagine a few of you out there were like me and experienced both. Friendship is beautiful and can be just what you need to see you through the worst, best, and the mundane times of life. I enjoy having friendships. I was never that person who was cool and had a lot of friends. For most of my adolescence, I think

I Am Joy

I was just tolerated by some people and I called them friends, but it was not truly friendship. Teenagerhood was a miserable, confusing time. I tried to navigate it as best as I could. Having said that, I was not always someone I would have wanted to befriend either. I was so starved for attention in my home, I would make up stories to try and get people interested in me. That always backfired, as lies typically do. Looking back now, I had no idea who I was, so trying to get other people to buy into some version of me was ill-fated from the start. Once I hit sophomore year in high school, things got a little better; I had a circle of people who I felt connected to, and that was all I really had wanted. It must have been difficult to be my friend. I was so lost, and hell bent on creating a facade around what my life really was. If I am totally honest, I really hated myself, and I couldn't even imagine people would want to be close to me. Nonetheless I did allow some people in, and in some cases that was a safe thing—but not always. I have such a vivid memory of being at my childhood home. It must have been a Friday or Saturday; it was a particularly good day. My sisters' friend had brought her baby boy over, and myself, mother, and father were all babysitting. I just loved every second of it. I remember feeling happy, and it was monumental because happiness and my home were not synonymous. Just as we were all laughing and enjoying this little boy, the doorbell rings, which was odd for anyone to just show up at our house. I answered the door and there stood three girls from school, who I described as friends then, but always knew they really weren't my friends. They were inviting me to a sleepover at one of their houses, which was only a few blocks over in my neighborhood. Reluctantly, I agreed to go. My thinking was that if I said no then they would never invite me again. So off we went walking in the dark, in the cold, to my friend's house. No sooner did we hit the end of my driveway I realized that this was not what I thought it would

Joy M. England

be. They walked off ahead of me, giggling and walking unreasonably quickly. I was alone, trailing behind them, desperately trying to figure out what I should do or say. As we approached her house, they slowed down, I thought, "Oh thank God, they are going to include me." My friend's house was perched on top of a very steep hill/driveway. We all stood at the bottom and looked up. Then, they looked at each other, turned to me, smirked and ran as fast as they could up the driveway and disappeared. It appeared that the entire purpose of the invitation was to show me in a very clear way that I was not a part of the group. After a few minutes, I turned around and walked home. As with many things in my life, the good moments always seemed to be eclipsed with some kind of trauma; friendship was no different. When I arrived home, my parents asked what happened. I don't remember what lie I told them. I just retreated to my room and cried for what seemed like days. Just another confirmation of the lie I believed about myself: I was not good enough. In all fairness, I don't remember if I knew why those girls were upset with me. It's quite possible I had told a story and embellished something and upset them. It could also just be that kids can be mean sometimes. I spent the rest of that weekend dreading Monday and the smirks and the snickering. I don't recall what Monday brought, all I know is I survived. I don't share this story to garner sympathy. I tell it set the background for how I ultimately understood friendship to be: conditional, scary, mean, and just out of my reach. I did go on to have some relationships in high school that I would call friendships that were of mutual respect and caring. They were few and far between, but I was so appreciative of them when they did happen. As a young adult, friendship changed for me. I became a different friend. I was changing, I didn't know I was, but I was starting to hate myself a bit less, which made it easier for me to be a real person for people to befriend. I remember the first best friend I ever had, post high school. we met at my first real job, Price Club. She was a good friend to me. She didn't judge me, she didn't deceive me, she truly cared for me. We rented what would be both of our first apartment and really just enjoyed being friends. She taught me so much about friendship, work ethic, being true to yourself, and honoring the people you love. I really loved her. We would remain friends for a long time—but when my life took a dark turn, and depression and illness ripped my world apart, our friendship suffered. She was the only person in my wedding party, and I was so grateful for her love for me, even though I couldn't show it. The magic of Facebook allows me to remain in contact with her albeit from a distance, and that's okay. I am so thankful that she is happy and healthy and living her best life.

Best friends are blessings, gifts from God to remind us how to love each other. If we are fortunate, we have an opportunity to have someone we call or called a best friend. Sometimes you are lucky enough for that person to be your best friend through all your phases of life, and sometimes that best friend crown changes heads over the years. I met a long time best friend in 2001. It has been a friendship journey of valleys and peaks, distance and closeness. What I have learned is that a true best friend, a God-ordered friendship, is destined to survive, and survive it will. I am so grateful for her friendship; she led me to God and has shown me what selfless love looks like. She was by my side when my daughter died and when I celebrated professional successes. One thing we always did was laugh together. We were a show stopping duo; laughter and good times encircled us. I could go on and on about the good times, the laughs, the inside jokes, the sideways looks that only we understood. Laughter is good for the soul; it raises your spirits without you even knowing. I am so grateful for the laughs and the great times. As any relationship, the times were not always good. There were hard times. We have not always treated each other with love; I was not always a great friend to her. Issues within my heart and spirit would not allow me to be a good friend many times. We spent many years apart, and I thought I could never forgive her for the acts I deemed unforgivable. Time and God have a way of softening hearts and bringing people back to each other. God has used sickness in both of our lives to unify us. I couldn't be more thankful for her in my life and the divine order of the timing of our friendship. Keisha, you have taught me immeasurably about faith, and God; I thank you from the depth of my heart for your love and friendship. #SoulSisters.

I have been blessed to have experienced friendships that were so awesome. Women need friends in this world. We need other strong women around us to lift us up when we need it, and check us when we are bugging. I have been blessed to have had those friends in my life. The funny thing about life is that we all have seasons. Not everyone is meant to remain through every season in your life. Some friends are for a specific season and distinct reason. I had a hard time with that. Because of my history of loss of people I loved, when I found a friend I wanted to hold on for dear life. Try as I might, seasons end, things change, and friends leave. The physical friendship may end, however, I carry with me the memory and lessons from those friendships always. I believe in my heart that you know who you are. Know I love you and I thank you for giving me the gift of friendship. I have shared some particularly troubling friendships in previous chapters; I would be remiss if I didn't elaborate, not to throw shade on anyone, or to judge anyone, but to really put a spotlight on how God used those people to evoke irrevocable change in me.

I have had two friends in my life that ended up engaging in a sexual relationship with my then husband. Two that I am aware of

— I Am Joy —

anyway. There is no way to sugar coat that—it is crappy. Regardless if I was the worst friend in the whole world, there are some lines that a person should just not cross. We have all heard the saying hurt people hurt people. I would like to add that hurt people attract hurt people. I was a very broken person. I was held together with dollar store scotch tape, y'all; it wasn't a good look for my mind or spirit. To say that I attracted friends who were broken in similar ways would be totally accurate. I often think I picked friends who I knew, subconsciously anyway, would betray me. When I was a new mom, I had befriended the girlfriend of male friend of mine. I thought she seemed safe; she was dating someone and seemed to be really interested in getting to know me. Whelp, I was wrong on every level. We became fast friends, which also became a theme in my life. We would spend time together and as couples. We all adored Owen and loved to be in his presence. At some point, I started to have the familiar feelings of something not being right. She would become a little meaner to me, a little more judgmental, and a lot more distant. Of course, D told me I was crazy and always looking for a problem. Let's fast forward. This friend, ultimately began dating my ex- brother in law and became the woman who eventually sat in my living room telling me she was taking over my life, family, and children. Clearly, we never had a friendship. Clearly, she had no idea how to be an upstanding person. Hurt people hurt people. A really big lesson that I think is so important for women, especially women with big calls on their life: jealousy is ugly and lethal. I couldn't see it then. I couldn't understand how anyone would be jealous of me, but the common thread of my failed friendships was jealousy. I couldn't see my shine, but other people could, and whether they were aware or not, they would do whatever they could to attempt to darken or eradicate that shine. Just because I couldn't see myself didn't mean that the world didn't see me. She saw me, she perceived me as a threat and an enemy, and she acted accordingly. All the love she professed for D seemed to immediately vanish when he was laying on that gurney in a hospital. Funny right? When times get tough, the weak will always retreat. In true fashion to my life, she went onto marry my ex-brother in law and co-parent my youngest niece. Awesome right?! I always thought, "Jesus, why can't I escape the perpetrators of my seemingly endless heartache?" I have learned that it's all divinely orchestrated, the good, the bad, and the self-induced. God will use every situation to our good. 'We know that, in all things, God works for the good of those who love him, who have been called according to his purpose,'(Romans 8:28). Needless to say, that friendship ended. And I went forward with my life, holding onto hate and rage towards her, D, my ex-brother in law, and anyone associated with them. The hate and rage lasted for so long, so very long, and I tried to convince myself I was over it, but I wasn't and wouldn't be delivered from that anger for a very long time. The glory to God, I was delivered. I have forgiven her, and myself. I don't know much about their lives now, but I do hope they have found peace and understanding of who they are and what they need in their lives.

 My deliverance in the friendship arena is ongoing. I was still operating from a place of hurt, so I fast tracked a friendship relationship with ANYONE who wanted to be my friend. Similar to dating, if you are not operating from a place of self-love and Godly confidence in who He says you are, then you allow desperation to take control. Desperation defined every relationship that I had. I was so starved for love and attention that I accepted and pursued any glimmer of attention. God had to bring me through many, many friendship trials and tests to get me to see where I was thinking and acting wrong. I had to learn to allow who God says I am to replace the fear and desperation of my flesh. The reality is we all want to share our lives with people, especially sharing the testimonies of our salvation. The catch is to make sure that we are sharing with love and let God tell us how we should be. I had to learn to pump the brakes and allow God to set the pace. I am not saying I operate from a place of not accepting new friends; I take my time and listen to my discernment when approaching any new relationship.

The stories of the women of the bible always fill me with amazement. The story of Ruth is no different. Ruth embodies all that I hope to be in my friendships; she embodies loyalty, fairness, dedication, and sacrifice. Ruth had a hard life; she was in the throes of grief and uncertainty. Her one friend, the one person whom she loved and admired, kept telling her to leave and go on with her life. Ruth never gave up, she never walked away. She trusted her friend, she loved her friend, she wanted to be the support to her even though I am sure she felt she needed supporting as well. Ruth really is the original Ride or Die friend. It paid off for Ruth. She listened to her internal leading. She knew that her friend knew of the love of God and she wanted to know more about it. She followed her friend to a land that didn't accept her but she persevered. She was obedient to her friend's direction, and in the end not only did she help to heal the broken heart of her friend, but God blessed her with one of the most beautiful love stories in the bible. I don't know about y'all, but I want to be that friend and reap the blessing that obedience sows.

My friendship evolution took a tremendous turn for the better when I found my sisters in Christ. Girl let me tell you! There is no friend like a friend who worships God with you. Can I get an AMEN!!! I love all of my sisters in Christ. I love them for who they are in the body of Christ. When I first was saved, I thought I had to be everyone's best friend at church; you don't and you should not try to be. As with any other relationship, some become your people, some become people you love from a distance. The difference for me with these relationships is that we have a common bond, a family blood that runs through our bodies from our Savior. That right there is a game changer! Ladies, let me tell you, go get you some sisters in Christ. I am not trying to paint a picture of women who are perfect and just always say and do the right thing. Sisters in Christ are still humans. We are flawed, we are broken, we are hurt BUT we are saved, and we are forgiven, and God knows we are trying as hard as we can to fight the enemy and be who God has called us to be. My sisters are blessings, and I pray for each of them every day. Some of my sisters in Christ have become my people, my prayer warriors, my encouragers, and my reminders of where I need to fix my eyes when life gets blinding. I am so grateful for my people. I have waited a long time for them. I have worked hard to be ready for them. I am amazed at the blessing that God has bestowed upon us all to be in each other's lives. To my #SoulSisters, ladies keep being the amazing women of God you are called to be, and thank you for choosing me to be in this sisterhood with you.

I AM 1 IN 4

PREGNANCY IS SUCH a miracle. Most of us take it for granted; we just think it is something that happens and then you get a beautiful baby. We think that way until we see the reality of just how precious pregnancy, fertility, and birth really is. Looking back, I understand just how truly blessed I was to have two healthy boys, given the state of my health and body. Nothing but God brought those boys to me. My baby girl, well she had a different call in this wonderful world.

Pregnancy for me was a bit traumatic. Shocking right? My first pregnancy was met with anger, disappointment, cruelty, and overall discontent. No one in my world wanted me to be pregnant, for a bunch

- I Am Joy -

of reasons, all of which were valid. Nonetheless I was pregnant. Everywhere I looked, people were upset at this miracle. D and my wonderful doctor were the only two who were positive and supportive. A time where we should have been celebrating, all I felt was judgement and hate. So needless to say, pregnancy started to feel like something I didn't deserve and should be shamed for. My second pregnancy was just as peppered with trauma. It was still not accepted, although not as openly rebuked as was my first pregnancy. My pregnancy with Nate occurred while D was on his destruction path, so there was no room for celebration as we were in the all too familiar state of just surviving. I look back now and feel such sadness for the woman I was in those years. I wanted so much to celebrate these babies that I felt so blessed to welcome. My world just didn't match my inner Joy. I did not have the skills at the time to really embrace my blessings. Nate came into the world, and he was just what I needed. I had my boys, and I knew in that moment that I would do whatever was necessary to be who they needed me to be. My third pregnancy, we had tried for a few months without success. It was a surprise on Labor Day 2007 to find out that I was expecting. I was so happy. I am sure you won't be surprised to hear that our circle was none too thrilled. Not outwardly hateful like before, but not in any way excited. This time around, I was working and had a much bigger circle of friends than I had ever had before. We felt supported by the few who shared our happiness. Internally, I was looking so forward to the celebratory things this pregnancy would bring: baby showers and maternity leave. I had never experienced any of these things; I was ecstatic to be on the brink. My pregnancy was going as pregnancies do: some discomfort, some sickness, and an abundance of joy and elation. My boys, especially Nate, were so excited. Nate talked to my belly every night before we went to sleep. I remember feeling like, "Okay, this is what we needed." I also remember distinctly thinking before I got pregnant that I was so miserable in my life and marriage that at least I could have another baby. D was good for that. I love being a mother. I love being pregnant—I wanted to feel that again. I felt stronger. Strong enough to say, "You know what? I am happy regardless of what my parents thought or felt." December 5, 2007. Owen's fifth birthday, I was having really bad headaches so we went to the doctor to see if all was okay. We got to hear the heartbeat, super strong at 154 beats per minute. Owen just smiled at the sound which made me melt. All seemed okay, and rest was ordered to ease the headaches. I remember feeling better the next day, and on December 7th 2007, we were off to the appointment all pregnant women look forward to: the anatomy scan! I was sitting in the waiting room, studying for a forensic psychology final and waiting for D and my mom to arrive. I was just so happy, I can't even think of another word. All the hateful self-talk was quiet, all the shame seemed to be subdued by the pride I felt carrying this baby. As I lay on the exam table awaiting the sonographer, I said to D what a great birthday present for him (yes, Owen and D birthdays are two days apart). The sonographer began her exam and abruptly dropped the scanner and left the room. I had been through enough scans to know this was not typical. I was panicking, my mom and D were panicking. I just kept saying, "No it's okay, I feel the baby moving. Thirty minutes later, the doctor came in and said, "I am so sorry, we lost this little one". My mother let out a primal scream like I have never heard in my life. We were all sobbing and screaming. It was the deepest devastation I have ever felt in my life. The doctor talked to us, but I have no recollection of what he said. In that moment, the wave of self-hate was back. All I heard was, "You see? You did this. You were too fat, too unhealthy, too horrible. You killed your baby." The shame came in tidal waves. I was drowning

- I Am Joy -

under the waves of hatred. How could this have happened? What did I do to deserve this? Was I really this horrible that I had killed my own baby? I had to get up and walk out of the medical office past exam and waiting rooms full of expectant mothers. Sobbing doesn't describe it; D basically carried me out of the office. We had to drive over to my OBGYN's office for the next steps. My mom drove me and D followed us. They were calling our friends and family telling them of the death. As we pulled into the parking lot, I remember thinking, "How am I going to walk in there? Everyone will know that I killed my baby." The shame crushed me. I got up and walked in. I was greeted with long faces of grief. These people had known me since I was eighteen-years-old. They supported me through my other pregnancies. They were hurting for us. God carried me down that long hallway to the doctor's office. I wasn't saved at this time. I didn't know God, but I know now that He carried me. I collapsed when my doctor entered the room. He comforted me, he apologized, he cried with us. There were instructions and choices. My doctor did all he could to guide us. A woman who just lost her child is in no place to understand or comprehend this information, so I just responded with what seemed like the least horrible option. So, with that we were sent to the hospital to have a D&C. I had no idea what a D&C was. All I knew was my other option was to wait for spontaneous labor and that seemed unimaginable. I was eighteen weeks pregnant, almost half way through, the law says a woman can have a D&C up to eighteen weeks. After that threshold, you must deliver your baby. I was told to go to day stay at the hospital. I was there with people who were having procedures like corn removal. We have to do better as a world,. When you are delivering your dead baby, the last thing you need is to be lumped together with people having minor procedures. When the elevator doors opened, my best friend was there. I just fell in to her arms and sobbed;

it was unbearable. No woman escapes this without losing who you were before. The next steps blurred some. I remember being given some medication to calm down, and to get my body ready. I remember my step-father coming in and kissing my head, then I was wheeled off. Upon entering the procedure room, they took my glasses, which renders me total sightless. I asked my doctor to please just do one more ultrasound; he agreed. The machine was too far for me to see anything—but there she was. I saw a perfect image, clear as could be. I told her I loved her and said goodbye. They knocked me out and I awoke without my baby. I awoke a different person; I would never be the Joy I was just four hours before. I was irrevocably changed. She was gone. They never told me if she was a she, but I believe with my everything that she was a she, and we named her Delaney. Delaney was the name I had chosen for a baby girl when I was sixteen; little did I know then that it means "Angel from heaven"—and boy is she ever. Explaining to a seven-year-old, four-year-old, and twelve-year-old that their sister and cousin was gone was torture. I don't know what I said, I just remember their faces. Sadness became all we knew. I had never really experienced the grief of loss before. I had lost people to death before, and I had grieved them, but this was different. This was a pain that I had never known before. I quickly became consumed with the loss. I identified with the loss; it devoured me. I kept going. I took a week off of work, and then I was back to my routine, and I finished the finals that I had been preparing for when she passed. Professors showed me compassion and empathy and I appreciated it immensely, but I knew I had to keep going. The darkness that covers you when you grieve is sneaky—it just snuck up and took over. I found myself spending countless hours watching YouTube videos of mothers who had lost their babies at eighteen weeks. The images were graphic, and the emotion intense, but I felt like I just had to watch. About two weeks after she died, I woke up to an image of a fork in the road. I heard very clearly, "You either choose to heal or you will succumb to this grief." I now know that was God talking to me, guiding me, literally showing me the choice in front of me. That day I found a grief counselor and started counseling. I was convinced that her death was my fault, my punishment for being a subpar human. As the genetic tests came back and confirmed her death was cord accident, it did not assuage my guilt and determination to blame myself. I was drowning in the waves of self-hate; I saw no way out from under this. I was miserable in every way you can be. I was in a dead marriage, I was not where I wanted to be professionally, I was still in college, I was overweight, I was unhealthy, and now I was the mother of a dead baby. I saw no way out of my own way. Everyone encouraged us to try again, which was bizarre to me given the history of people not wanting me to be pregnant. Now everyone wanted me to be pregnant. I felt a shift in me; I knew I wanted more children, but I also just kept feeling like not now, not with D, this is not what I want. Within six months of her death, I left D for good. I kicked him out of the house after receiving a phone call from one of his girlfriends that said to me, "I know all about you, your boys, and your dead baby." In that moment, I knew that I needed out of this marriage and no matter how scared I was, I was brave enough to leave. Delaney blessed the boys and I with freedom. Our little angel who was brave enough to fulfill her purpose in this life to save her family. Ten years later, I still feel her loss. I still feel her with me. I know she's watching us, and I believe she is proud. Delaney was my blessing born from my deepest misery. I am so thankful for her life and her death as I know now that she fulfilled her call in life. What more can a mother ask for? Until I see you again beautiful baby, I love you with all I have.

— Joy M. England —

I AM NOT MY NUMBERS

NUMBERS CAN BE some of the most condemning and prison-creating things in this world. I guess if we give power to something, then it has the ability to control and imprison us. For me, what feels like my whole life is filled with dreaded numbers. As a teenager/young woman, my head was filled with the number on the scale. I remember the first time that I ever really realized that the number I was seeing was a bad one. Don't get me wrong, I was painfully aware my whole life that my body was not good, not acceptable, not what a "normal" body should be. However, this next story is regarding my mind and spirit attaching to a number on the scale, a number that would become my arch enemy. Picture your standard high school gym, full of teenage angst and hormones. There we all were, lined up in several rows, and at the front of the gym were the gym teachers. I was at the back of the line, so I couldn't really see what was happening. I was thinking, "Ugh, they are putting us in teams," for some sport that I would likely not have any aptitude for. I wish that is what it was!! To my horror, as I neared closer to the front of the gym, that's when I saw it: the eighteen-foot-tall scale! Okay, it was just a regular doctor's office grade scale, but it seemed to me to be eighteen-feet-tall at least. My second horrifying realization was that they were not just weighing us, they were yelling out the weights to the data collector on the other side. If I could have sprinted I would have. I wanted to die right there in that spot. Mortified doesn't begin to describe the feeling as they called us one by one up to what might as well have been an executioner. Nothing stopped time as I stood there shaking and contemplating what my new name would be when I changed my identity and fled for Mexico, I heard, "Joy, your turn.: CRAP!!! I would be lying if I said I didn't contemplate spontaneous fit of tears to avoid this fate. In what seemed like the slowest of slow motion moments, I walked up and got on the

— I Am Joy —

damn scale. I looked to weight announcer with merciful eyes, begged in a soundless display for her to drop dead so she wouldn't yell my weight across the gym. No matter my hopes for death on this poor woman, she didn't drop dead. She lived, and seemed like used her biggest, loudest voice to scream 164 across the gym. I think I might have stopped breathing for a few minutes as I walked back towards my peers (I say peers, because friends were not something I had much of in high school, especially not the beginning of sophomore year). So, there it was, a number that I would learn to hate. Three digits that summed up all my flaws, all my inadequacies. I don't recall anyone saying one word to me, no snickers, no nasty comments. I attribute that to a few things. No one cared because they were facing their own fate at the top of the line. Secondly, 164 is not that bad, therefore not warranting a response from anyone. If only I could have told myself that, then. It amazes me to this day how we have the ability to turn a non-moment into a life-defining moment. I would go to work every day, in terribly unhealthy ways, to never see that 164 again; ironically, that 164 number would become my goal number as an adult. Still holding onto numbers, letting go of that is where the real work comes in. I would love to report that this was the only time in my life where numbers ruled my thinking and defined my worth. Sadly, that's not the way the story goes. Numbers of many types would infiltrate my thinking over the remaining years of high school, however the scale was the laser beam focus. So, I manage to escape high school, relatively unscathed. I distinctly remember feeling like I was finally free, free of the people who had shown me such hate, free of the prison of my home life, free of the teachers and administrators with power trip issues. I would quickly realize I was anything but free.

Numbers would come to rule my adult life. Constant measuring of weight, pants size, college grades, and then of course bills and income.

Joy M. England

Numbers were everywhere I looked, I could not escape them, there was no parole; I was trapped for life. Due to my unhealthy relationship with numbers, and all the power and control I surrendered to them, my adult life would quickly become quicksand that would pull me down to my neck and keep me there, right on the verge of total take over. How we define ourselves, or better yet what we allow to define us is such an important foundation. We all know the parable of building your house on sand versus solid ground. The shiftier and more unstable your foundation, the weaker and more vulnerable your house will be. I was operating from a house that was built on a sinkhole; I really had no chance to keep my house standing. I quickly began to see myself as nothing more than a number. I was out of high school about a year when I got sick—that's when the number game hit epic proportions. I lost control over the one thing I had been relatively good and controlling my weight. I went from a "normal" weight to obese in thirty days. Thanks PCOS, for being the bully you really are. I gained sixty-five pounds in thirty days when I turned nineteen-years-old. Those were some sucky numbers, for real for real. Those sixty-five pounds I would carry with me for all of my twenties and the majority of my thirties. Along with the gift of PCOS also came high blood pressure and diabetes. Anyone who has experienced, or knows someone with diabetes, your life becomes your numbers. You literally start your days with a prick to the finger that collects a minuscule drop of blood that a machine reads and tells you if you are good or bad. Well, my numbers were always bad, most often described as horrible. For me, this was just confirmation of the piece of crap person I had believed so deeply that I had become. My life was now using the scale and the blood-sugar-demon machine confirming for me that I was indeed all the things I had ever heard or believed I was. I was a failure, disgusting, unworthy, sick, undisciplined, good for nothing, fat, and overall a waste of space. We all go through phases in our lives where we are ruled by something. We relent and allow the something to become the main thing, and we lose ourselves in the process. I was lost. Joy had left the building in every possible way she could. To add insult to the already damaged existence I was living, I went on to make horrible financial choices, time and time again. I can give you all the reasons and the perfect storm that led to those horrible decisions. The important thing to know is that because I had shaky sinkhole for a foundation, my house never stood a chance. I was empty inside, I was in a marriage that I hated, I hated myself, I loved my children, and they provided the only comfort I would have in this life I felt so trapped in. My other comforts came in the form of food and spending. I shopped and spent money in an attempt to fill the sinkhole. Spoiler alert: that doesn't work. I would shop and buy the boys things or do what I could to make the house/apartment that I was living in look pretty and put together. It was like hanging a picture on a burning building and hoping no one will smell the smoke. I had no skills; I had no idea how to cope with the pain of my life and the grief I felt over the life I thought I would have. So, I succumbed to the numbers. I would consciously think, "Well you are already fat, your diabetes is already out of control, your credit is shot and bank account is empty already, so why not take this bill money and go to Applebee's? At least that would numb the pain." The funny thing about coping skills is that we will create good healthy ones and ridiculously unhealthy maladaptive ones, and those are the hardest to let go of. Once I had salvation and a growing relationship with God and had put in some serious work on address each and every of those maladaptive coping skills, I would learn that they were really hard to let go of. It's like throwing your binky out the window on the highway at eighty-miles-per-hour. I felt like I was being disloyal to abandon the thinking and beliefs that I felt had kept me alive all these long, sad, and traumatic years. When do we learn to outgrow those ill-fitting coping skills and put on the skills that fit us nice and make our butts look good?

I AM SLEEVED

THERE ARE ALL kinds of side effects that plague a person who has low self-worth and even lower self-esteem. For me, the deadliest side effect of my abysmal self-esteem was that I stopped caring altogether about what happened to me. I developed this terror of bad medical news and or judgement from doctors. Since the inception of my illness, I had been in the presence of medical professionals, some of whom were deemed "experts" in their respective fields, however they clearly missed the rotation in bedside manner and compassion. Before I realized it, I was in full blown shame of all things medical. I had morphed from someone who had these medical anomalies happening to her to someone who was at fault for the anomalies and somehow not worthy of even basic respect. Don't get me wrong, I am so grateful for the dozens of medical professionals who have treated, encouraged, and saved my life. I am forever indebted to the teams who supported me through some of the darkest times. I guess you can't have the good experiences without the bad ones—and I definitely had some bad ones. Sickness is scary, sickness is traumatizing, and sickness is also something that changes you. When you are chronically sick, it can easily start to shape all areas of your life. I began to resent myself and the doctors who I was supposed to be able to trust. Who knew there was such a thing as White Coat Syndrome? Well let me tell y'all, it is a real thing, and it is zero fun. I had gathered up all these terrible medical reports, and more gloom filled prognoses than one person should ever have and turned them into a wicked case of anxiety and utter avoid-

- I Am Joy -

ance. That's basically what White Coat Syndrome is: anxiety attacks as soon as someone in a white lab coat walks in the room. To this day, I struggle with the sight of white coats and lab results. In early 2016, I made the decision to pursue bariatric surgery, the Gastric Sleeve to be precise. This surgery had the potential to cure my diabetes that was ravaging my body and drastically shortening my life expectancy. I was excited at the prospect of having a smaller shape, but mostly was so ready to be free of needle sticks, pills, and more needles. In April 2016, after returning from a business trip, I found myself battling what would be the scariest medical emergency of my life. That is saying a lot considering I had brain surgery in 2011, but I digress. I was home maybe twelve hours and had no choice but to drive myself to the emergency room. The pain was excruciating, and I had no idea what I was about to face. The diagnosis was severe pancreatitis, which was brought on by extremely high cholesterol and triglycerides, which was brought on by uncontrolled diabetes. So, that was a mouth full. What does it all mean? My uncontrolled diabetes caused my cholesterol and triglycerides to be so high that it basically gunked up my pancreas' ability to function. It was pain like nothing I had ever experienced; not even childbirth compared. So there I lay in a hospital bed on narcotics that could take a horse down in my veins, and I was still unable to function through the pain. I remained in the hospital for two weeks with pseudo-cysts covering my internal organs. Sounds fun right? I was released from the hospital and sent home to continue recovering, which took an additional six weeks. This, my friends, was a life changing experience. If you don't heed the warnings your body gives you, and the whispers God speaks to you, God will do what He needs to get you still and quiet. Well God, you got my attention, and I will work every day to never take my body for granted like that again. Within a few months of this ordeal, I was cleared for Gastric Sleeve surgery which would happen on September 13, 2016. My miracle day,

— Joy M. England —

one of my many rebirths. Within about forty-eight hours of surgery, my blood sugars began to normalize, and within three months I was off of all diabetes medications. Praise Jesus! Surgery is always tough, but recovering from bariatric surgery physically wasn't too difficult—mentally that was another story. I did hit a complication from my surgery about five weeks post op: a stomach leak which landed me back in the hospital. Enter White Coat syndrome level epic. The hospital stay post stomach leak was traumatic. It was highlighted by a doctor who helped me tremendously but also ignited a new level of fear of doctors. He was horrible and brilliant—the brilliant means less when you treat people terribly. Nonetheless, I am grateful that it was repaired and went on to recover wonderfully. Praise Jesus! I love my sleeve. It is a tool, and it is a reminder at times of what I went through. I am not ashamed of my surgery. People judge it and I couldn't care less. I am proud of the body and mind that has survived more than most and is still here encouraging, empowering, and leading people to be the best versions of themselves they can be.

This experience has taught me so much about myself and what I am capable of. It also brought me face to face with my images of self-hate and disgust. I spent my entire life hating my body—all versions of it. I also spent my entire adult life hating my weight, obsessing over my weight, dieting, and failing. My weight determined whether or not I was worthy of love, friendship, and whether I was a capable mother. There were so many times in my life people, usually family or people close to me, would use my weight as another reason why I sucked. This one particular time stands out above most. It was a hot August day. I forget the year, but I was still married, and my boys were small, maybe five and three. We were invited to a friend's daughter's birthday party. We were very close to this friend and his two kids; they were even with us at the memorial following Delaney's death. I loved the little girl we were celebrating. She was a fighter. She had a chronic

- I Am Joy -

illness, and I think that is what bonded me to her so much. I felt like I could relate to where she was in life and how doctors and numbers ruled her life too. So here we are on the way to the party that was being held at her mother's house. I had never met her mother, as she was an alcoholic and not in the kids' lives often. I remembered how horrible getting dressed was for any day, especially summer because I hated everything about how I looked. So, on that day I was only comfortable in long pants and a long-sleeved shirt. Crazy in the August heat, but that was my life. I remember enjoying the party and enjoying celebrating the kids. There was a moment when the birthday girl's brother was upset, and I went to console him. I guess that was a trigger for his mom and she began to verbally attack me. I had no skills to defend myself from the name calling and shaming that flowed from her mouth. I walked away with my head down, with my kids and my husband who said nothing at all in defense of me. I remember getting into the car feeling like a worthless person. It was that worthless feeling that surrounded me my whole life; it was an old friend to me. Every now and again, that same friend visits. For the most part, the weight loss that I accomplished after my sleeve did give me a sense of pride and self-worth that I had not had any other time in my life. Unfortunately, changing on the outside does not always manifest a change on the inside. So those old thoughts of, "You are ugly and not good enough," creep back in and I start to judge myself on, "Did you gain weight back? What do you look like? What do your labs say?" It's a viscous mental cycle. Thankfully, the changes that I needed to the inside were available to me the whole time, I just needed to recognize the causes of the pain and then accept what needed to be done to heal them. All in all, my sleeve is my friend. My sleeve was a first step in a long journey of rebirths and resurrections.

4

I Am Saved

Accepting salvation is the best gift I have ever received. I was saved in June of 2014. For those of my dear friends who don't know what it means when someone says they were saved, I will explain. Christians believe that salvation occurs when you accept Jesus as your Lord and Savior and profess that with your mouth. Out in the open you say that you accept Him, and whammo you are saved! Thank you, Jesus, that salvation is user friendly. I attended a church where I was blessed to receive the word of God and lead by pastors who allowed themselves as vessels for the creation of disciples. That proclamation, that moment in time, that public confession of an inward acceptance is a life changer of epic proportions. I was filled with hope and encouragement. I finally felt like I wasn't alone. God restored my Joy in the months following my salvation; at the time I had no idea that it was the Joy of God. I just knew that I was so flipping happy! Salvation is amazing and necessary; however, it does not magically erase all of your human issues or fears. Salvation takes effort on our part. We have to remain chasing our calling over our fleshly desires;

it's hard work, and not for the faint of heart. Fleshly is another church term; I was in church for a minute before I understood that they were not referring to someone's physical flesh. When we speak of our flesh, we are referring to our human desires, needs, actions, wants, and previous (or still current) sin. Humans. We want what we want, and we like to do the things that feel good. Many times in the walk with Jesus, we have to let go of these fleshly desires because we are now called to do the works of God, not of our own personal wants. A lot of times, the fleshly wants are absolutely not in line with the Word or Will of God; newly saved folks have a tough time with the battle of the flesh—at least I did. It is hard to reconcile this love that you feel in your heart and soul for the savior that you just accepted into your heart with the autopilot settings of your mind and body. As with anything in life that really matters, it requires hard work—salvation is no different. My salvation took seed in my spirit slowly. It was watered by good shepherds who taught me the word of God. It is so important that you keep learning as you walk with God after you have been saved. You need a strong foundation of understanding His word and the call He has for your life. I loved church, I loved worshipping, I loved hearing the word of God and watching people give their lives over to Him Sunday after Sunday. I may not have had a relationship with God my entire life, but I was always a believer, and whether I realized it or not, I was so filled with faith in God. All believers who are saved are blessed with faith in God; I truly believe that some of us are blessed with a gift of faith. Much like we all pray, but some of us are prayer warriors, I feel the same way about faith. I, my friends, am one of those believers who are gifted with faith. Let me explain why I proclaim this. As I mentioned, I have always believed in God. I always prayed, and I always hoped that there was better out there for me. What kept me going all those dark years, all those years when many would have

- Joy M. England -

thrown in the towel, I kept going I kept pushing. I refer to this earlier as this small voice that I would hear in my mind that would say, "Keep going. There is more. There is better." That still small voice was always God, igniting my faith, reminding me that I am destined, showing me that even through the darkest of dark nights, there is always a dawn; there are fresh mercies every day. I have a very brilliant memory of a time in my life where I thought it really could not get any darker, and then God sent me an angel that showed me that faith is all the light you will ever need. It was the dead of winter, Owen was about 3 years old, and Nathanial was an infant of maybe five months of age. D and I had been staying at my sister's home, and something happened. I have zero idea what the traumatic event was, but she kicked me and the boys out into the cold, snow-filled streets. I had no job, no money, no car, and nowhere to go. I had no way of reaching D, who was at work. So with Nathanial in his car seat carrier and Owen holding my hand with one hand and his beloved bag of dinosaurs and cars in the other hand, we started walking. I remember being so cold and feeling so ashamed that I was in this position that my boys were suffering in such a way. Of everything that I had endured in my life, this was the worst moment. So, we walked, and I tried to sing songs to Owen to distract him from telling me how cold he was. As we were walking, a car came to a stop beside us, asking me if I wanted a ride. I respectfully declined and said we were fine. The woman insisted and said her house was right around the corner, to please get the babies out of the cold. Everything in my mind yelled stranger danger, but I accepted her offer and got my boys in from the cold. We arrived at her home; it was lovely, and peaceful. She warmed Nathanial's bottle for me and Owen took to playing with her granddaughter. I was so relieved to be in from the cold and in the presence of someone who clearly did not mean us any harm. She didn't ask me any questions, and there were no judgements about how we ended up there. She just talked to us, she held Nathanial, and he just loved on her. It was a kindness I had never ever known. I felt like I had known her for years. She shared with me that she was currently undergoing treatment for breast cancer, and I was so astonished that this woman who was enduring so much reached a helping hand out to me, of all people. She never brought up God or faith to me. She didn't have to; it radiated from her. I saw the cross in her home, and I immediately prayed thank you God for bringing me to her. She was an example to me, even though at the time I didn't realize the spiritual magnitude of that encounter. There are angels of God everywhere. We each have the opportunity every day to be what this woman was to me. Days later, I took what little money I had and bought a thank you card and mailed it to her. I pray that she was met with the same kindness in life that she showed me. She encouraged my faith, and I am not sure how to express my gratitude for that other than honoring it by emulating it in my life. Faith has brought me through everything in my life, and it became even more present in my life when I accepted Jesus. I have gone on in my life to take leaps of faith repeatedly; it has become somewhat of a theme for my life. Many women have said to me over the course of my most recent years, "Your faith has inspired me to do and try." That is the most amazing gift I could ever receive. Faith can be scary, but more times than not, it is absolutely peaceful. 'Faith is confidence in what we hope for and assurance about what we do not see' (Hebrews 11:1). I spent my whole entire life not being able to see the light at the end of the tunnel. I spent so much time in the dark that when the light shined, it took me a minute to adjust. What I know clearly know now is that I needed to spend those years in the dark. I needed to feel the helplessness of depending on myself. Because it was those years that strengthened my faith, that showed me that I am never the one to depend on; all my dependence comes from my faith. I have confidence now in my future because that future is already written. The dark days come, and the leaps of faith feel like jumping off a million-mile-high mountains blindfolded. Having faith doesn't remove the hard times, and it doesn't take away the fear of leaping. Absolutely not. What it does do is fill you with the confidence that no matter what is unseen, we are covered and protected. There is no better feeling than knowing that placing your trust in God allows you to have the peace that what will be will be, and all things will be used for your good.

When I was newly saved, it was a battle of mighty wills. I wanted salvation, I believed strongly in the God who saves, but my flesh, as church folk say, was not happy about his new year new me nonsense. My path to salvation and walking in faith was nothing short of miraculous divine intervention. My salvation is what finally allowed me to heal from the abandonment I felt my entire life. Let's recap; my childhood was filled with pivotal moments in time where I metabolized life's events as rejection and abandonment, and I went on to marry a man who would eventually confirm those same ideations. Shall we not forget the men that came after my marriage and tattooed "not good enough" on my forehead. Throw in extended family and friends over the course of my life who, to my interpretation, said a big peace out to me when I needed them; and I was convinced that I was inherently not good enough and not worthy of love, especially not loving myself. Only time, maturity, grief, therapy, and God would open my eyes to the lessons in the loss that would write my future and provide me with the eyes to see the tools I had all along. TGBTG! (To God Be the Glory).

I was walking in salvation for about three years when I decided to get baptized. I did that a little backwards, but hey, I never did do things the way everyone else did. My baptism came at a time in my life where I had taken the biggest leap of faith I had ever imagined. I wasn't totally sure why I felt so called to baptism at the time I did, but there was no doubt in my mind that now was when I was supposed to do it. Baptism for me was the next step in my faith walk. I wanted to be literally washed from my previous sins; I wanted to start the new life that I was so devoted to. God was and remains my everything. What better way to express that love than in a public display of my commitment to God? The water of baptism washes away your sin. You raise up from the water anew. I couldn't wait to experience it.

I AM FAITHFUL & DESTINED

FAITH IS ONE of those terms that people throw around casually. Faith is certainly not something to casually toss around. Faith is clearly defined for us in the bible. Here is what God tells us faith is. 'Faith is the assurance of things hoped for, the conviction of things not seen' (Hebrews 11:1). My go to version of this verse is the New Living Translation. Faith is the confidence that what we hope for will actually happen; it gives us assurance about the things we cannot see. That's a great verse, isn't it? I just fell so in love with that verse. I love the peace it invokes in my heart and mind. God's promises to us are beautiful and purposeful and to be treasured. Well, then life happens. Life gets hard, and the walk with God gets hard. That's when the meaning of faith because more intense. Faith doesn't work without obedience and discipline. Obedience and discipline, for me anyway, don't invoke feelings of peace. Those words used to cause me to shift into a full-blown grown up temper tantrum. God had to work with me to show me that obedience and discipline can be wonderfully calming assets to our emotional skills libraries. As a person who accepted salvation, I was

— Joy M. England —

by default blessed with a degree of faith. You have to faith in order to profess and proclaim Jesus as your savior. However, that faith you are given as a baby Christian is not enough to sustain your journey with God. Like most things in life, we need to practice it in order to get better at it—faith is no different at all. Faith takes commitment, studying, fellowship, practice, obedience, and discipline. Sounds like something you aren't running to jump after, right? Let me share with you my faith journey to date. I am pretty confident it will change how you view the sacrifice of faith.

When I was pregnant with my first son, I remember thinking as I was preparing for his birth how amazing it would be to meet my new son, and that life would just be as beautiful as every Pampers commercial for newborn diapers portrays. Then you actually birth that first baby and get the "pleasure" of experiencing all the things that the Pampers commercial leaves out—and there are many things they leave out. You then begin to realize that this miraculous love you feel is coupled with some of the most terrifying and difficult things you have ever experienced. For a long time, I would think regularly, "How can I be simultaneously loving every second of this moment and also be dreading that this beautiful little person will throw my entire day off track?" Well ladies and gentlemen, faith is very similar. It's a miraculous love to accept Jesus and embrace our faith in Him and the word of God. As you grow more and more aware of the power that is salvation, you also start to see that with that growth comes pain, sacrifice, trouble, and stress. Faith doesn't promise you will never struggle or you will never hurt. Faith guarantees that when you face those pains, you won't face them alone, like you did before salvation. We can all relate to really just wanting something so badly that it can easily consume your thoughts, day, nights, and before you know it, your actions and reactions are centered around this one thing. If you have never felt this way at least once or twice in your life, then we may need to check and make sure you are conscious. For me, I felt this so many times in my life, both before and after salvation. The difference is after salvation when your faith is in something above your own ability, the recovery from the obsession is easier. Also, you get this amazing gift of healing in the process. I am sure you are reading this like, "Is she trying to talk us into or out of faith?" Bear with me, I am going somewhere great with this. The human experience is wrought with pain and failure, both necessary for change and growth. As humans, we wander around our lives trying to define who we are, where we are going, and what the purpose of our lives are. I would argue this is all normal and necessary parts of the human experience. Along the way, we pick up some tools that are not helpful—and typically not all that pleasant. Some of us pick up addiction; I picked up addiction to wanting to be liked and needed. Some of us pick up denial; I denied that I had any issues. Some of us pick up avoidance or lying; I avoided being who I knew I really was because of fear of judgement and ridicule. So I would lie to others and myself in an attempt to be who I thought they wanted me to be, so that definition of Joy would change with the audience. Any of these relatable to you, or I am out here on dysfunction island all alone? At the height of my maladaptation and total misguided view of myself and my world, I still had faith. I didn't call it faith in God. I would likely have defined it as a hope that things would turn around. I always believed in God, loosely, but I had no relation and no real faith because you can't be faith filled (truly faith filled) and non-believing at the same time. So, I flailed around dysfunction island, sometimes thinking, "Ha! I have got this under control. I am hidden, and the Joy I think people want to see is exposed and on display," while the real Joy was bound and gagged and dying for attention. My fear to was too great to allow any faith to seep in deep where it was needed. Fear, as I have learned is poison that will erode any chance you have for real change and growth. Fear poisons your mind, thoughts, words, actions, and reactions, rendering you powerless. Fear is something we need to learn to respect, because it has power and is necessary in some forms, like the fear of God, the human fear we have developed over our lives is our enemy and we need to treat it as such. If we want to be faithful in our lives, our relationships, ourselves, we need to learn to check fear at the door. Let me share with you some of the ways fear ruled over my faith and how in the end (spoiler alert!) faith won!

Fear was my homegirl for the majority of my life. We were inseparable. In the good times, the bad times, the regular times, fear was there with me taking my hand and leading the way. If I wasn't with fear, or giving into fear, I didn't know how to be. So, I stayed with fear. It was painful, and most times I hated my homegirl, but she was what I knew, so beside her is where I remained. As a child I learned that fear was the focus of my world. I was either in fear of what would come or in fear of what would happen after. Fear was the ruler and its rule was relentless. I watched how different people reacted to fear; some would scream against it, some would shrink from it and disappear, others would just remain indifferent to it, as if it wasnt standing there screaming at them. At some point, I decided that my way of facing and handling the fear was to avoid and pretend. I was terrified all my life, of one thing or another, one person or another. I dragged that terror with me in to my adult life, marriage, motherhood, career, friendships—it was with me everywhere. I didn't recognize it as fear until very recently. When something is such a huge part of us, we just learn to accept it and don't try and figure out if it belongs there. Fear took up all the prime real estate in my mind and soul. Fear defined me, so I never had to. Salvation changed all this;

I Am Joy

salvation saved me from me. Don't get me wrong, I didn't profess Jesus as my Lord and bam! all my fear was gone. I wish!! That is not how God works, He needs to bring you the ability to really see what's missing in inside you. That requires a new sight and that takes time and work. I think people envision a scared person as someone who ceases to exist in their life, right? That's so not how fear manifested in my life. In essence, I did fail to exist, because I was not being who Joy really was; I was only letting her out in small doses to the people who I thought wouldn't judge her, and those were very few. On the day to day, I was present in my life. I was reaching for goals, I was raising my boys, I was trying to navigate marriage, I was moving along in life. I wasn't sitting in a dark room waiting for the day to be over. I was in fear so deep that it didn't even occur to me that I was afraid, and that, my friends, is cause for real terror. In order to change that thinking, I first had to realize that I was operating from a place of fear. Think of a time that you were afraid, like physically afraid. Maybe when you almost rear ended a car, or you almost fell down the stairs. If you are like me, immediately after the initial threat subsides, your body begins to remind you that it is scared. You may shake or sweat or cry. It's a physical release of the terror your mind and body just endured; it's a normal and necessary release. For those of us who live in a state of fear, we never get that release. We are always walking around still in the initial reaction. We are jumpy and on edge; we are emotionally preparing for impact over and over again. We don't ever get to release the tension that the fear causes. It goes without saying that can't be good for us mentally or physically. I tried everything I could to ease that physical manifestation of the emotional state of fear: shopping, eating, working, accomplishing goals, and nothing worked. It never could have worked because I was trying to ease symptoms and wasn't addressing the real problem. I look back now and I feel sorry

- Joy M. England -

for the little girl who learned so early on that fear was normal. My heart breaks for the little girl who couldn't find her way out of the terror, so she internalized it and tried to be its friend in hopes that it would stop bullying her. Now that little girl has so much peace. She is free to be the Joy she always knew was inside of her. Today I honor her and all her glory because she did everything she knew how to do to survive until she could find salvation. Salvation saved me from the survival mode that fear put me in. Survival is a mindset that will be never ending cycle if left to its own devices, a cycle of surviving pain, life, relationships, and never thriving. I often described my life when asked as "I'm surviving." How sad. It is a sad fact that fear imprisons you in survival mode, which then keeps you from really truly taking risks because you feel like you can't risk your safety, emotional or otherwise, for a dream or a hope; you have to focus on the task at hand: surviving. The biggest problem with survival mode is that it distorts your senses and makes you think that you are in immediate danger and therefore must just address the basic needs and forfeit anything bigger than that. What's a more effective way to crush faith and dreams than to convince yourself it would be life-threatening to focus on anything except your immediate (self-perceived) peril? I might be one of the more extreme examples of someone who is living in fear, but I know that it is more common than most of us think it is. I was saved for over four years before God really truly took me through a test that would once and for all rip fear from my grasps and show me that I need to grab onto faith, and I would need two hands to do that. I think at the core of my fear was my fear to be who I am. Since I internalized my early life experiences as, "Joy, you are innately wrong, unwanted, and unworthy," I became a young adult and adult who was terrified to show myself and my beliefs to the world because I believed who I was, was fundamentally flawed. Breaking free of that fear would be one the single hardest things I have done in my life to date. The breakthrough happened four years after I was saved, and about two weeks before am writing this chapter today. This break away from fear came when I was the most faith filled I had been in my walk with Christ. It is no coincidence that the trial came at my height of faith, because it would take every ounce of that faith to survive the fire required to burn free from the fear that gripped me my entire life. Sounds dramatic right? Well, that's because it was dramatic and traumatic. Walking with God and having faith in His power to save and heal doesn't mean it won't hurt sometimes. I had to break free of something I had held onto so tightly for forty years. That is bound to hurt. Breaking free with God means that even when the pain is unbearable you have a promise that God will never forsake you. He goes before you and beside you. God brought me through the fire, the fire that required me to open my mouth and be me, face the truth, and declare that I am good enough, my opinion matters, my choices are sound, and that I love me no matter what mistakes or shortcomings are in my rearview or in my future. That Joy is defined by God and not by my family of origin, my mistakes, or my generational curses. I am fearfully and wonderfully made. I refuse to fear rejection, judgement, and strife any more. I am free from the chains of shame, and that freedom was bought at the highest price on that cross in Calvary. God used those fears to burn me free of a life of surviving and set me on solid ground to live a life of hope and faith.

Learning to accept yourself, release fear, and your past hurts is the easy part, believe it or not! The real work, the real faith, the real eye-opening discovery, happens when we embark on pursuing the big F word. Nope, not that F word. I am talking about the real F word: Forgiveness. Christian or not, forgiveness is hard. It is some of the hardest work I have done in my life. Pain is hard, trauma is hard,

Joy M. England

rejection is hard, but it all pales in comparison to forgiveness. We have all heard the wonderful antidote that forgiveness is for you, not for the person you are forgiving. It's true, totally unequivocally true. Forgiveness is necessary; without it, you stay stunted right where you are. You can't go around it, you can't push it down, you have to face it head on and finally forgive the who, the what, and the why of your pain. You are likely thinking what I thought when therapists, pastors, friends, and spiritual leaders told me, "Joy you need to forgive." How do I do that? I wish I could tell you there is a magical algorithm for forgiveness—there isn't. There are pointers, there are sure fire ways that will lead you to successful, life changing forgiveness, but there is no one-size-fits-all-do-this-and-you-will-forgive potion. As you learn to begin to really pull back the layers to all that unforgiveness you have been schlepping around, you will see that it seems to go on forever. Just when you think you have turned a corner, and you are about to slap the "I climbed Mount Unforgiveness" sticker on your proverbial bumper, God will show you just how much more work you need to do. Here is the real truth my friends: forgiveness is ongoing. I compare it to this notion: if you want muscles, you have to do the work, consistently. What a total bummer for people like me who don't exactly call the gym bae. Once I realized that it's really true, you need to consistently exercise in order to reap the benefits, I came to see the same is true of forgiveness. Forgiveness begins with revelation. I found that I was carrying things that I had no idea where there. Here are the things that help me continually climb Mount Unforgiveness. Prayer and surrender were key for me; allowing God to reveal to you the areas that you need to shine some light on is paramount for the endurance you will need to sustain forgiveness. We all have our stories that are comprised of the good, the bad, the terrible, and the amazing. All parts are important; learning to honor your pain is fundamental for forgiving, especially for forgiving yourself. When we honor something, it becomes impossible to simultaneously hate that same thing. Your journey in this life shapes you. You are never given more than you were built to endure. Be grateful for that hard stuff, give it a huge high five. It's those things that catapulted you into the destiny of the world changing, world conquering person you are today. One of the most difficult times in my life centered around a grief that I wouldn't wish on anyone. This life event triggered immense self-hate. I had never felt more like a failure then I did at this moment in time. It would take years to learn that this moment in time was needed. It was destined. It was what I needed in order to develop the skills to forgive all the tragedies in my life. Surviving the loss of my daughter when she was just eighteen weeks along, losing her as I was growing her in my womb, was the hardest most devastating thing in my life. It was also the destined event that shot my life onto a new track that would lead me to writing this book today.

    I have held many titles in my life that I never thought I would hold: mother, graduate, entrepreneur, leader, author, faith warrior, and woman of God just to name a few. All in all, here I sit, an accomplished woman of God who is honored to be called a mother to more boys than I physically birthed, a leader to those in search of their voice, and a business owner to a company committed to empowerment and encouragement. God has a funny way of grabbing you right in the middle of your mess and showing you that there is triumph in the tragedy and wisdom in the sorrow. After all, when we are destined, even our free will can't shake us from what we are called to be. Your calling is just that—yours. I implore you to take a look at what you haven't forgiven, what you have survived, and where you feel like you have failed, because you are likely to find your destiny buried deep in the darkness. Life gives us the chance to use our God-given tools to

– Joy M. England –

turn oppositions into opportunities. Recognizing what your tools are can be difficult. We are so conditioned to believe the lie that we don't have the skills, and we are not worthy of the good works our hearts dream of. I am here to tell you the tools are there. Everything you need is already inside of you. When my boys were little, they used to love these little toy capsules. The capsule package proclaimed that with a little water (and a lot of patience) this capsule would transform into a whole, complete figure. The first time my boys experienced this, they just thought it was the most miraculous event. After a good amount of time deciding which was the BEST package (did we want dinosaurs or zoo animals? My friends, this was an epic decision for a four and six-year-old), eventually we decided both were the best. With our capsules chosen, and our newest play friend about to be in our hands, we rushed home and hurriedly opened the package, filled the cup with the recommended amount of water, dropped in our capsules and waited. All three of us watched with wide eyes, waiting for the transformation. As the minutes ticked by, our spirits began to wane, and worry settled in. My boys started asking questions like, "Mommy, did we do it wrong?" and, "Mommy I think mine is broken!"; I was a bit worried they might be right. Things were not happening as we had expected. We thought for sure that we had done the right thing, so why didn't we have the result of the whole figure? So, as any good mom does, I read the instructions after we realized we might have done it wrong. As I read the instructions out loud, I stated the steps with confidence that we had fulfilled the steps correctly and in the right order, and then, there it was in size two font, "transformation may take up to 72 hours." WHAT!!!! What kind of mean spirited, vindictive person creates a toy that makes a kid wait 72 hours to play with it?! Man, oh man was that a room filled with long faces. They stayed around for a few minutes just watching their cups, waiting desperately for their new friend to emerge from inside their capsule. I am not sure who was more disappointed, me or them. The three of us kept circling back throughout the day with hopeful hearts. As our cups sat on the kitchen counter, in clear sight, we waited and watched for two days. Just as we collectively began to give up, there was the emergence. On top of all three cups were three floating figures: two dinosaurs and a giraffe. Hallelujah! We were elated, even though we doubted that the capsules had what it needed on the inside to break through. All it took was time, and the friends we had waited for emerged from their dark capsules. The same is so true for us. The wait for transformation can seem like the longest wait of our lives; but at the end of the day, we have everything we need on the inside. Just like our capsule friends, it just takes the appropriate amount of time for us to emerge whole. If we can keep believing and hold onto our confidence, then we can allow God to do the work that will cause for our emergence to be everything we ever dreamed it would be.

When we accept that we are destined, then what? How do we define what our personal destiny or call is? I guess we can all define it a bit differently. For me, I define destined as a predetermined course, that no matter how off course you veer, you will always realign on the course. Just as things can be destined to fail, they can be destined to succeed. No one escapes the journey of life without ups and downs. Your bravery is built during your struggles and sorrows. So even though we don't hope for the downs, we need them, so we have the strength for the ups. If I would have been asked when I was nineteen what I was destined for, I honestly have no idea what I would have said. Probably something about college, about marriage, and about kids. If you had asked me at thirty-five what I was called for, I probably would have said singleness and struggle. If you had asked me at thirty-nine, I would have told you singleness and professional success. If

– Joy M. England –

you asked me now, I would tell you amazement beyond my wildest dreams. A common lie that I think most, if not all, of us fall victim to at points in our lives is the lie that success looks just one way. As if there is only one way in this life to succeed, and if you choose differently, then you suddenly become destined to fail. My particular path to what the world would call success looked nothing at all like what everyone expected it to look like. When I graduated high school, I knew I wanted to attend college. It wasn't ever a maybe; it was always a definite. I selected to attend community college after high school. I was never ever talked to about or encouraged to pursue a traditional four-year college experience. I was salty about that for years, but I see now that how my life rolled out was exactly how it needed to. I loved community college, it was there that I experienced freedom I had never known; it was also there that I began to see that in life you have to be able to count on yourself. Shortly after graduating high school, I entered the workforce full time, met my future husband, and started collecting experiences and knowledge that would mold me into my future self. I didn't take a traditional education path in many ways. I attended community college for about eleven years. Say what! I know, let me explain. I pursued my undergraduate degree through a communiversity program that allowed me to get a state university education (go Rutgers) at a community college. This was ideal for me because I was a wife, mother, and full-time employee the majority of my undergraduate tenure. I had many things that attempted to thwart my educational goals: sickness, divorce, births, deaths, low self-worth, just to name a few. I am so grateful that I believed in myself just enough to keep pushing through. I graduated with my undergraduate degree from Rutgers University in May of 2011. I was so amazed at my accomplishment. I was astonished that a day I thought would never come, came! There I was in my cap and gown, walking across the stage to accept a degree that represented more than I realized it did at the time. That degree symbolizes perseverance, it symbolizes bravery, and it was one of the first times where I had some proof that all the lies I believed about myself maybe were not true; I had seen something through. I wasn't a failure. Something I have learned over the course of my life is that figuring out what you are destined for is not at all as important as accepting and believing that you are in fact destined. I know I am destined to continue to do amazing work in the Kingdom of God. I have no doubt at all about that. I don't know exactly what that work will look like, or how it will take shape, and that is not really important to me. What remains the most important part about destiny is your faith. Remember that your story, your journey, those ups and downs, are all part of the roadmap to your predetermined call. Enjoy the ride! Keep pushing forward, allow people to lead you, and then return the favor by leading someone else. Be fierce about your destiny. Keep it centered on your vision board of life. You have a unique purpose in this world, and only you can accomplish what you were destined for.

I AM JOY

Everyone encounters a time in their lives where they have a crisis of identity. I think for most of us this happens repeatedly over our life spans. As we grow, we change how we define ourselves. Although some pieces of us are just us, no matter what else we change, some things will always remain as constant descriptors. We must learn to make sure those unchanging descriptors are positive, God-given descriptions. As a child, I was so saddened by all things that were me, that I developed a hatred for my very name. I would ask my mom why she picked my name. I despised it for so long. When I was in high school, I even researched how to legally change your name. That was commitment back then—there was no Google. I had to physically go to the library and search for books in the card catalogue. Your girl was knee deep in the Dewey Decimal system for days. When I look back now, I see how much I had no idea who Joy was that I rejected myself down to my very name. I can say to you with confidence now that I love my name, I embrace my name, I am proud to be Joy and all that entails. We all need to learn to embrace who we are, even if we are still actively believing the lies people have spoken over us that cause us to think we are unworthy and damaged beyond repair. It is a process to learn ourselves, to recover from the wrong perceptions we have believed for so long. Part of that recovery is self-acceptance. We all aren't called to everything: accepting ourselves means to accept what we aren't as well. I often tell leaders when I am training them, "There are some things I can teach you, and there are others that you either have or don't have." The realization of what you may or may not have built within you can be a tough mirror to look into; as with all the tough stuff in life, that is usually where the greatness is born. Living a life where you don't know how to define yourself is a natural part of development. Staying stuck in the Who I Am I's is where the danger comes in. If I were to describe who I am to you right now in this moment, I would say gracefully broken.

    Let's talk labels for a moment. Sheesh, have I had quite a few labels over the years. I have learned to peel the labels off, but not to discard them completely. Why you ask? I will tell you. I use my old labels as reminders, reminders of what God has healed, and a reminder of what I do not want to return to. The key to this exercise is to not hold onto the labels as accurate or current descriptors, but to honor them as part of the path that lead you to the healing-seeking badass you are today. I don't drag my labels around with me. They don't get to enjoy all the

I Am Joy

amazingness that is my life on most days. They are neatly packed up in a bag, tucked away for good. I dig through the bag every now and again. Life has a funny way of knocking you around so you feel like you have to pull out old labels to cover up a new wound. I am here to tell you that is not what your decarded labels are for. Take a moment and visualize something with me. You can do it. EnVogue told us to Free Our Minds, and we all know that anything we were told in the 90s must be good for us. So free your mind, just for a moment and visualize yourself as a blank slate. A blank cardboard cutout of you where all you can see are the features of your face. Now start putting on your old labels. Throw them on there like a magnet on the fridge. Dig up those oldies but goodies that we like to slap on ourselves as soon as we start to feel anything other than good. Keep going, keep slapping those labels on there. Some might be huge labels; others might be the small tiny ones. They all matter, and they all take up space, so get them on there. Be honest with yourself, only you and your spirit can see this so don't be bashful. Once you think you have gotten all those old labels on there pretty completely, I want you to pick a new color for the lettering and start putting your current labels on the big cutout of yourself. If you are like me, this is hard to do; there is not much room left. Where can you squeeze in the current when the old has all the prime real estate? Now we are left with some labels that have no place to go. That sucks right? We can't rep the person we are today when we are too busy being the person the world or our families and friends told us we were before. So, grab a bag and start pulling off those old labels. Tuck them away in a bag that you can dig through when you need to honor where you came from, but far enough away that it won't clutter up the prime real estate that is you. If you are anything like me, your cardboard cutout was tipping over under the weight of my labels. My sleeker 2018 version of my cutout is much lighter and easier to maneuver. The real work comes in when we are pulling off those old labels to reveal the space for our new labels. It is kin to when I would tell my boys it was time to dwindle down the toy collection. They would spend hours digging through their toy chests, just to realize that they couldn't bear to part with anything. They would look up at me with long faces and say, "But mommy, they are all my favorites. They are all important." How do we part with something that is so important to us, that has literally defined us emotionally for years? Well the truth is, sometimes we can ceremoniously say goodbye and part ways, and sometimes we just need to chuck it in the goodbye bag and lick our wounds later. It is not easy work my friends, but it is the most important work you can do.

How I would define myself today still changes regularly. We are humans, and humans are filled with emotions and reactions to the experiences of life. All those experiences and reactions change us; they mold us into the us we are becoming. Like forgiveness, who we are becoming is also something that needs our daily attention. Let's talk examples of this daily requirement that I speak of! As a leader in my professional life as well as my personal life, I have one go to question that I ask people when they feel they are at a crossroads with a decision in their lives. What is your three-to-five-year plan for your life (professional or personal) and does this choice you are making point in the direction of the goal or away from it? This was the question is asked myself when I was focused in school and my career. It wouldn't be until years later that I would be able to apply that question to my personal life. If nothing else, this question would cause people to pause and refocus how they were approaching their current dilemma or opportunity. Does this align with my goals? Does this align with where I feel God is calling me to go? Does this align with my mission, both personal or professional? Distractions come in many shapes and

I Am Joy

forms, and if we are not careful, what looks like and smells like a great opportunity could just be a distraction that pull us from our paths. If we don't take the time to take inventory of who we truly are and what we want to accomplish, then we put ourselves at risk for missing the opportunities that can catapult us into our destiny as well. Writing this book is a great example of this point. There was no point in my life that I ever thought, "Wow, I am going to write a book." I am book nerd of epic proportions (and proud of it!) but being an author was never something I ever placed on my three-to-five-year plan, or any plan for that matter. Life will teach you that sometimes your best laid plans will never come to pass. God will show you better than He can tell you that His plan will kick your plan's butt any day. So here I am writing a memoir of sorts, a book that I believe will lead women to Jesus, a book that was always written in God's plan for me. So, I had to add it to my three-to-five-year plan. I had to adapt my current plans to include opportunities as they presented themselves, even though I had zero confidence when I started that I would ever be able to write anything. Be flexible with your plan; be diligent and focused. Here is what I know for sure: keep planning, keep striving, keep asking yourself, "Does this align with where I am trying to go? And if it doesn't align, could it be an opportunity that I had never thought of but would be beneficial to my life goals?" To all my believers out there in book reading land, for you I say pray about it. Keep praying, keep asking, and listen for the answer. God will tell you what direction you should go, He is faithful to answer us always.

 At forty-one, I would define Joy as a work in progress. I am a woman who is honoring her past, embracing my current mistakes, acknowledging my accomplishments, and striving to be who I am called to be. I am intentional in my relationships. I am kind to myself. I am open with my faith. I am the voice of the little girl who had no voice. I am

- *Joy M. England* -

the friend I always wanted to have. I am the mother that my boys need me to be. I am the leader that my company, clients, and staff need. I am a daughter of God. I listen and, more importantly, obey what God needs me to do in His kingdom. I am striving to be all I was planned to be. I am preparing to be the godly wife that I am called to be. I am preparing to be a published author. I am accepting who I am: the good, the bad, and the ugly. I am Joy and I love and honor that.

End

Knowing Who You Are by Dr. Marshall Davis is a masterpiece. This work is an essentially powerful compilation of consistently riveting principles, teachings and decrees that will establish the reader in such a way to remove the doubt and insecurities that each one of us face daily. The blessing in the reading will interrupt and disrupt patterns of pain, offense, frustrations, delays and even failures. This reader highly recommends this literary work as a foundational part of every church library and bible study curriculum. Dr. Davis' closing remarks in the summary is compelling...'God Bless Your Knowing'!

Pastor Vivian Foster,
VOC Ministries Int'l Inc.

Dr. Marshall Davis offers powerful, yet simplistic strategies to readers that help us understand who we really are based on biblical principles. **Knowing Who You Are** *acts as a significant resource of empowerment for all who struggle with self-image, self-awareness and self-perceptions. It skillfully redirects negative self-talk into positive and insightful affirmations that develop the ability to elevate and strengthen confidence in who we are as God intended. This book helps us to see ourselves as God sees us! It provides us with the tools necessary to identify areas that have acted as mental barriers, emotional triggers and spiritual strongholds resulting in deeply embedded self-sabotaging behaviors that consistently work sub-consciously against God's divine plan for our lives. In short, Dr. Davis' book,* **Knowing Who We Are**, *is a book of deliverance that makes God's Word relevant generating the results of success within areas always needed and desired, but never before experienced.*

Dr. Pepper Martin
Senior Pastor of the Destiny House Christian Center